# Backroads of
# Vancouver Island
# and the Gulf Islands

# BACK ROADS
## VANCOUVER ISLAND
### and the GULF ISLANDS

## JOAN DONALDSON-YARMEY

LONE
PINE

**The Publisher: *Lone Pine Publishing***

| | | |
|---|---|---|
| 206, 10426 – 81 Ave. | 202A, 1110 Seymour St. | 1901 Raymond Ave. SW, Suite C |
| Edmonton, AB T6E 1X5 | Vancouver, BC V6B 3N3 | Renton, WA 98055 |
| Canada | Canada | USA |

**Canadian Cataloguing in Publication Data**
Donaldson-Yarmey, Joan, 1949-
  Backroads of Vancouver Island

  Includes bibliographical references and index.
  ISBN 1-55105-099-4

  1. Vancouver Island (B.C.)—Guidebooks. 2. Gulf Islands (B.C.)—Guidebooks.
3. Automobile travel—British Columbia—Vancouver Island—Guidebooks.
4. Automobile travel—British Columbia—Gulf Islands—Guidebooks. I. Title.
FC3844.2.D66 1998          917.11'2044          C98-910216-5
F1089.V3D66 1998

Senior Editor: *Nancy Foulds*
Editorial: *Volker Bodegom*
Production Manager: *David Dodge*
Layout & Production: *Beata Kurpinski, Gregory Brown*
Book Design: *Beata Kurpinski*
Cover Design: *Gregory Brown*
Cover Photographs: *Al Harvey, David Dodge, Joan Donaldson-Yarmey*
Photography: *Joan Donaldson-Yarmey, Al Harvey, David Dodge,
        Volker Bodegom, Witold Kurpinski*
Cartography: *Volker Bodegom, Gregory Brown*
Printing: *Transcontinental Printing, Toronto, Ontario, Canada*

The publisher gratefully acknowledges the support of the Department of Canadian Heritage.

# CONTENTS

*Dedication*

*To Elizabeth, Terry and Sarah*

# Acknowledgements

Like most of the people whom I have met on my travels, the residents of Vancouver Island are friendly, polite and helpful. As anywhere, you may meet the occasional disgruntled person, but these experiences will only add to your harvest of stories from your trip.

I would like to thank the people who work in the tourist information booths for answering my questions and for giving me directions. Also, my thanks go out to the people at the attractions and museums who corrected my misunderstandings about the history of their area, and to the employees of the many small grocery stores who did their best to help me to find the places that I was looking for.

I would also like to thank the staff at Lone Publishing for the wonderful job they did on editing, layout, maps and cover on this book and my other two BC books, *Backroads of Southern Interior British Columbia* and *Backroads of British Columbia's Lower Mainland*.

A special 'thank you' is owed to my editor, Volker Bodegom, for his knowledge of when more information was needed, for his finding my many mistakes, for the contribution of his own information, for his attention to detail and for his patience while working on this book and on the two books mentioned above.

Many thanks to my husband Metro (Mike) for his total support.

# Introduction

You can spend days driving through British Columbia without ever tiring of the changing scenery. From snowcapped mountains to deep-blue lakes, from bald eagles to black bears, from casting for that trophy fish to hiking through the forest, this province has something to offer everyone driving its roads.

The best part about travelling on Vancouver Island is that you are never far from the ocean. As you drive along the east coast, you can see the waters of the Strait of Georgia most of the way. And, because Vancouver Island is long and narrow, you can travel relatively quickly via paved highways and gravel roads to reach its west coast. The Inland Island Highway, opened in 1997, has been designed to whisk you to your destination in record time. But if you take it, you will miss the best that Vancouver Island has to offer. Therefore, this book takes you along the older Island Highway—and sometimes on the even older original Island Highway—as you head northwards up the east coast.

*Mortimer Spit, South Pender*

The well-travelled highways of British Columbia are paved, but once you get off that pavement, you are on gravel roads. *Backroads of Vancouver Island and the Gulf Islands* takes you down many of the backroads worth exploring in the far southwestern corner of the province that is not part of the mainland. And, in addition to covering Vancouver Island itself all the way from the Saanich Peninsula to Cape Scott and from the Strait of Georgia to the Pacific Ocean, it also takes you to the renowned Gulf Islands and introduces numerous lesser-known islands as well.

Visit as many of these smaller islands as you can, because each one has a unique beauty and a unique history. Maximize your enjoyment by taking into account what

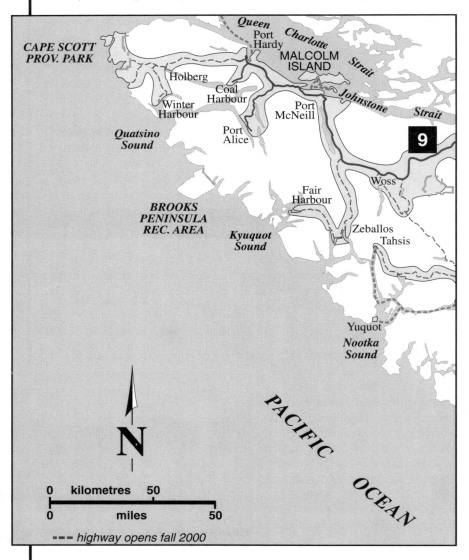

facilities and amenities—especially accommodation—are and are not available on each island you plan to visit.

This book gives you an idea of what there is to see and do on each road, but it does not claim to tell everything, so feel free to explore any other public side road that you see and to make your own discoveries.

*Backroads of Vancouver Island and the Gulf Islands* is divided into sections that could mostly be driven in a day—or you could tarry along the way and set a more leisurely pace. Chapter 4, which includes the Southern Gulf Islands, is an exception, because of the ferry schedules. Each chapter is as closely connected to the next as

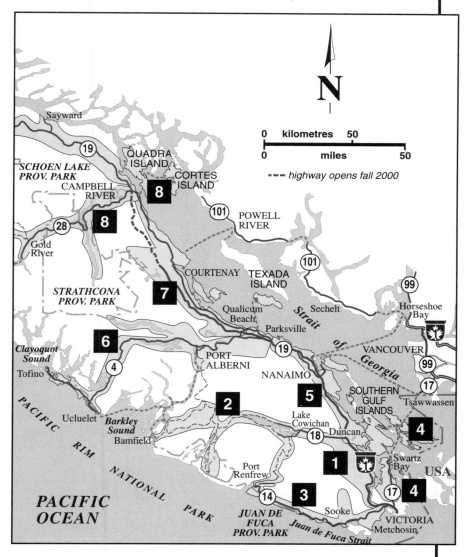

possible, to make travelling easy and enjoyable.

There is a map at the beginning of each chapter to give you an idea of how the route is laid out and where to find its highlights. However, the intrepid backroad explorer will want to acquire additional, more detailed maps such as the BC Forest Service's Forest Recreation Maps (free), the 1:250,000 and 1:50,000 topographic maps from Geological Survey of Canada, the Discover British Columbia series from International Travel Maps, recreational atlases and locally produced maps.

Most of the gravel roads in this book can be travelled by car or by motorhome; those that are not suitable for certain kinds of vehicles are noted. However, as you will be driving up and down many hills, make sure that your vehicle is in good condition,

*Butchart Gardens*

especially if you are pulling a trailer. Also bear in mind that gasoline, supplies, repair services and medical care are less accessible once you get away from town and off the major highways.

The gravel roads that you will be driving have generally been constructed by the forestry industry for use by their logging trucks and equipment (though some are for mine access). Logging trucks, when full of logs, can weigh up to 90 tonnes (100 tons) and take up the whole road. The trucks in the bush usually have a larger, wider load than those seen on the highway and they drive more slowly, especially uphill. They also create a lot of dust, which lowers visibility.

Logging roads are often only one lane wide—the truck drivers are in radio communication with a dispatcher who tells them where to pull over to let oncoming trucks pass. You, on the other hand, have to remain alert and be prepared to yield to logging trucks—keep track of the pull-outs you pass just in case you have to back up into one to let a logging truck go by. Be sure to travel with your lights on at all times and keep to your side of the road.

Longer logs sometimes stick out behind the logging truck—they are called 'sweepers' because they can sweep your car off the road if the truck passes you on a curve. Therefore, make sure that you are in a safe place, well off to the side, when you meet a logging truck or when you park along the road.

Roads that lead to villages or attractions are usually open to the public. While most other logging roads can be driven with caution at any time, some might have a sign stating that they are 'active,' which means that you should keep off, unless the sign says that you can use it at certain times. If a sign says 'deactivated,' it means that the forestry companies are no longer maintaining the road. It could be in bad shape and should not be driven. You are advised to check with the nearest tourist information booth or the forestry companies for road conditions and logging activity before attempting the more out-of-the-way routes.

While maps put out by logging companies may name every road, that does not mean that there will be road signs once you get there. Therefore, the measured distances and landmarks mentioned in the text are often all that you will have to navigate by.

As some roads are closed down, new ones are cut into the forest. In addition, bridge wash-outs, snowfall, rockslides and falling trees can close a road for a short time or a long time, especially during the stormier, darker months. These changes can cause problems to people who are expecting to reach a destination or to visit a certain attraction. Therefore, anyone driving on logging roads should be on the lookout for new roads and unexpected obstacles and should be prepared to modify their plans at a moment's notice, even if it means driving all the way back the way they came.

There are plenty of provincial parks and beaches to enjoy, and only some of them are mentioned in this book, just to give you a few ideas about where to have lunch or to camp for the night. Beachcombing, picnicking, swimming and relaxing are a few of the activities that you can do at most any public lakeshore or oceanside.

One of the bonuses of backroad travel is the free forest service recreation sites along them. They are provided courtesy of the logging industry for tourist use. However, all are 'primitive,' meaning that there are few if any amenities beyond an outhouse and a couple of picnic tables if you are lucky, and you are asked to take out all your garbage when you leave. They all operate on a 'first come, first served' basis. You can, however, reserve ahead for the private campgrounds and for some of the government ones—for provincial parks, call 604-689-9025 (Vancouver) or 1-800-689-9025.

Hikers, take note that because of BC's rugged terrain, many hiking trails have steep sections, most of which are mentioned in the text. Be certain that you are in good enough shape for the climb before starting out, and that you are properly prepared for the kind of hiking that you plan to do, even if the weather suddenly changes.

If you plan to do any clam-digging, fishing, hunting, power boating or searching for historical artifacts,

*East Point Hippo, Saturna Island*

do check the regulations in effect and acquire any necessary licences, so as to protect BC's resources and to avoid legal problems.

The province of BC is full of scenic hideaways. All are well worth the effort that it sometimes takes to reach them, so pack up, get out and enjoy!

*Whippletree Junction*

# THE MALAHAT
# to LAKE COWICHAN

This route will take you along the western side of Saanich Inlet, which separates the Saanich Peninsula from the rest of Vancouver Island. You will see where the Canadian Pacific Railway's 'real' final spike was driven by Sir John A. Macdonald, visit 'the City of Totems' and end up at one of the largest lakes on Vancouver Island.

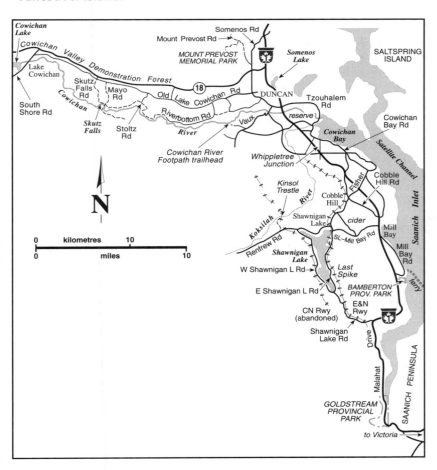

# The Malahat to Whippletree Junction

## THE MALAHAT DRIVE & MILL BAY

'Mile Zero' of the 7821-kilometre (4860-mile) Trans-Canada Highway is at Beacon Hill Park in Victoria. The highway was begun in 1952 and completed in 1962 at a cost of $1 billion. Said to be the longest paved highway in the world, it extends across Canada's ten provinces, ending in St. John's, Newfoundland.

Head west and north out of Victoria on Highway 1, the Island Highway. When you pass the Goldstream Provincial Park campground on your left, look for the sign that states, 'start of Malahat Drive,' which marks the beginning of the climb to the Malahat Summit. Shortly after the sign you come to the Goldstream Provincial Park's picnic area and visitors centre.

Goldstream Park is the site of Vancouver Island's first grist (grain) mill and its first sawmill. Later, in 1885, gold was discovered here and it was called 'Gold Creek' by the first prospector in the area, Peter Leech (also see the section on Sooke and Leechtown in Chapter 3).

In 11.2 kilometres (7.0 miles) from the Malahat sign, you come to Shawnigan Lake Road on your left. It goes to the southern end of Shawnigan Lake and from there the East Shawnigan Lake Road follows the eastern side of the lake to the village of Shawnigan Lake while the West Shawnigan Lake Road goes along the other side of the lake.

**The Goldstream Trail** In the early days, travel from Victoria to the settlements farther north was by boat. Each settlement had a dock where supplies were unloaded and passengers disembarked. A few roads ran from the dock to the nearby farms. After many complaints about the lack of an overland route, the government built the Goldstream Trail, west of the present highway, in 1861. It extended from Victoria to Cowichan Bay. Just 1.5 metres (5 feet) wide, it was suitable only for riding horseback, walking or driving cattle. The government promised that it would be widened the next year.

However, it was not until 1884 that the Goldstream Trail actually became a rough wagon trail. In the early 1900s, again after complaints—this time of fallen trees and floods—a new road was begun over the Malahat Ridge. In this 16-kilometre (10-mile) stretch, 123 culverts were put in and 18 bridges built. It opened in 1911.

Continuing northwards on Highway 1, 2 kilometres (1.2 miles) past Shawnigan Lake Road, you reach the Malahat Summit, with an elevation of 352 metres (1155 feet). At the summit there is a viewpoint where you can look out over Finlayson Arm, Saanich Inlet and across the water at the Saanich Peninsula. There are other viewpoints as you begin descending. The best one is at the rest area, from where you can see the farms and the streets of the Saanich Peninsula.

At kilometre 19.2 (mile 11.9) from its start, you reach the end of the Malahat Drive section of Highway 1. Then, just past that point, take the right turn to Mill Bay and Bamberton Provincial Park. You are now on Mill Bay Road, part of the original Island Highway. It carries along the ocean shore for 5 kilometres (3 miles) to Mill

Bay. (If you do not take Mill Bay Road and stay on Highway 1, you will nevertheless reach Mill Bay, in 3 kilometres (1.8 miles) from the junction.)

Watch for seals out in Satellite Channel. Early in the morning and at dusk are when they like to climb onto the floats and docks.

One of the first sawmills on Vancouver Island was built at Mill Bay in 1861. On the north shore of Mill Bay, at Whisky Point, a young 'Al Capone' made his money by selling rum and whisky to the islanders during Prohibition.

When you reach Highway 1 again, turn right and then, when you get to the set of traffic lights at Shawnigan Lake-Mill Bay Road, turn left to go to the northern end of Shawnigan Lake.

If you appreciate apple cider, watch for Cameron-Taggart Road at kilometre 2.2 (mile 1.4). Turn right and drive 1.9 kilometres (1.2 miles) to Merridale Road, where you turn right again. Follow this road to the end, where you will find the Merridale Ciderworks, the only ciderworks on the island. Here you can buy cider in any size from a half-litre to a keg. It is open Monday to Saturday between 10:30 AM and 4:30 PM.

## SHAWNIGAN LAKE

Continuing along Shawnigan Lake-Mill Bay Road, in 5.3 kilometres (3.3 miles) from Highway 1 you arrive at a flashing light and four-way stop in the village of Shawnigan Lake. To see where 'the Last Spike' in the railway system across Canada was driven, turn to the left to follow Shawnigan Lake Road alongside the lake. At kilometre 2.4 (mile 1.5), keep right at the Y to stay on Shawnigan Lake Road. It becomes a very narrow road with residences on both sides.

At kilometre 4.3 (mile 2.6) from the flashing light, you reach Cliffside Road. Find a parking spot on the road here and walk up Cliffside Road, as there is no parking farther up. At the top there is a small circular area with driveways leading off it. Follow the driveway that is straight ahead (actually a narrow road) and goes uphill. When you get to the top of that hill, you can see the railway tracks to your left. It is a bit of a climb to get to them but once on them, turn to your left and begin walking.

*Shawnigan Lake*

In about 100 metres (330 feet), you come to a cairn on the right side of the tracks. The plaque on the cairn reads:

> *August 13, 1886, the Last Spike was driven on the E&N Railway*
> *by Sir John A. Macdonald.*

The Esquimalt and Nanaimo Railway (E&N), constructed by the Canadian Pacific Railway, ran from Victoria to Nanaimo with a stop here at Shawnigan Lake.

Back at the flashing light and four-way stop in the village of Shawnigan Lake, go straight through and follow the road as it curves and crosses the railway tracks. When you reach a Y in the road, go to the left, onto Renfrew Road. At kilometre 6.8 (mile 4.2) from the flashing light, turn right onto Gleneagle (or Glen Eagle) Road.

Half a kilometre (0.3 mile) from the turn onto Gleneagle Road, take a road to your right and immediately afterwards turn left onto the gravel road that runs parallel to Gleneagle Road. You are now on the old railway

Last Spike cairn

bed of a spur line of the E&N. Follow it to where large rocks have been placed across it to keep the traffic out.

Park here and make the half-kilometre (0.3 mile) walk to the Kinsol Trestle over the Koksilah River Valley. This structure is one of the highest and longest wooden trestles in the world. It was built to provide railway access to the King Solomon Mine, which once operated here.

The near end of the trestle has been destroyed, so you cannot walk onto it. That you cannot do so might be a good thing, since the trestle is flat, with no sides, and you can see how it is way above the valley as it curves to the left. To explore farther, you can take one of the paths down through the trees alongside of it.

Go back to Renfrew Road, which as the name suggests, used to go to Port Renfrew. The road has been closed part-way since 1984 because of a bridge in bad repair. However, you can still travel along it as far as the bridge, though there is nothing special to see, apart from some scenery.

**Wineries** *If you travel Highway 1 from Mill Bay to Duncan, watch for the winery signs. At these wineries you can take guided tours of the estates and sample their wines, which are growing in popularity. There are three in the Cobble Hill area and two in the Duncan area.*

## COBBLE HILL AND COWICHAN BAY

Turn left off Gleneagle Road onto Renfrew Road and drive to Shawnigan Lake Road, which is just after you recross the railway tracks. To go to the village of Cobble Hill, turn left onto Shawnigan Lake Road. In about 3.8 kilometres (2.4 miles), keep left as the road joins Cobble Hill Road. In short order, pass Hutchison Road and then turn right on Fisher Road to enter the village.

If you are here on a Sunday, visit the flea market, 'the Swap and Shop.' It is located in the Farmers' Institute Hall, on the corner of Fisher and Watson roads. This hall is also the site of the oldest annual fall fair on Vancouver Island, held on the third weekend in August.

Get back onto Cobble Hill Road and head northwards to cross Highway 1. Now on Cowichan Bay Road, continue onwards to visit the seaside village of Cowichan Bay and the Marine Ecology Station, where you can see British Columbia's marine life in numerous aquaria. It is at Pier 66 on the waterfront and it is open from noon to 5 PM every day during the summer and on weekends only in the spring and fall.

On the other side of town, continue to the northwest along Cowichan Bay Road. Once you pass Hecate Park, look for a pull-out on your left 2.4 kilometres (1.5 miles) down the road. There are a number of plaques here: one honours the first white settlers, who arrived here in 1862; another is to Robert Service, who worked in the area before going to the Yukon; and a third is for the pioneer women of the area.

*Kinsol Trestle*

## 'The Butter Church'

*The Stone Church on the Cowichan Indian Reserve was originally called 'St. Ann's Church.' Built in 1864 under the direction of Father Peter Rondeault, it is the second of four churches in this area named for St. Ann. The very first of these churches was built with logs in the 1850s. The Stone Church received the nickname 'the Butter Church' because Father Rondeault paid his helpers with butter that he had churned from cream milked from his two cows. However, this church was used for services for ten years only. There are two stories as to why it was open for such a short time: one is that the owners of the land wanted it closed down and the other is that the church officials decided that the church should be on church property.*

*When the third St. Ann's Church was constructed up the road, the Butter Church, with its tall steeple, was renamed 'the Stone Church.' A few years later, the third St. Ann's was destroyed by fire and a fourth one was built in its place.*

*The walls of the Stone Church were made from stone laid on stone until they stood 9.1 metres (30 feet) high at the gable ends and were 0.6 metres (2 feet) thick. The church was built by a stonemason from Victoria, helped by the Comiaken Natives.*

*The hill that the church sits on was called Kla-ouw-tan by the Natives before the coming of the Europeans.*

*You can visit the church if you get the Cowichan Band's permission.*

When you get to the junction 0.5 kilometre (0.3 mile) past the pull-out, look to your left. The South Cowichan Lawn Tennis Club, the second oldest lawn tennis club in the British Commonwealth—Wimbledon was the first—celebrated its 110th birthday in 1997. This court is one of the few remaining grass courts in the world and it will always be grass, because if it is ever covered with asphalt, the property will revert to the heirs of the family who donated the land.

From here, turn around and drive 1.8 kilometres (1.1 miles) back to Hillbank Road and turn right. Turn right again when you reach Highway 1. (As an alternative, if you kept on going along Cowichan Bay Road, you could take Tzouhalem Road through the Cowichan Indian Reserve on your way to Duncan, passing 'the Butter Church' about 2 kilometres (1.2 miles) north of Cowichan Bay Road.)

## WHIPPLETREE JUNCTION

Drive northwards on Highway 1 from the junction at Hillbank Road and watch for the sign marking the right turn into Whippletree Junction. There are a few buildings along the highway, but go behind them to the town square, where there are many more. Standing in the square and looking at the buildings almost makes you feel as if you have been transported back to the early 1900s. Take your time as you wander through the general store, the shops that sell artifacts, antiques, crafts and gifts, the barber shop and other specialty stores.

This reconstruction of an early 1900s village began in 1971 when a man named Randolf Streit salvaged unwanted buildings from Duncan's Chinatown and rebuilt them here. The Whippletree Junction General Store, for instance, was formerly a restaurant in Duncan's Chinatown. Other buildings have come from Cobble Hill and Sooke.

*Whippletree Junction*

On the left, just 0.5 kilometre (0.3 mile) up the highway from Whippletree Junction, is the World of Wonders Wildlife Park. This park features many animals, birds and reptiles from Canada and around the world. For instance, you can see snakes, bison and chameleons, in reconstructions of their natural habitats. The park is open from 10 AM to 5 PM every day.

Then, on the right, at kilometre 2.4 (mile 1.5) from World of Wonders, you can stop in at the Old Farm Market to get some fresh vegetables for your supper.

# Duncan to Youbou

## DUNCAN & AREA

In 1886 the settlers in this area asked that a railway station be built on the land of William C. Duncan, through whose property the railway ran. When that request was granted, they laid out a townsite. The name of this little community was changed from 'Duncan's Farm' to 'Alderley,' and then to 'Duncan's Crossing,' 'Duncan's Station' and 'Duncan's.' Finally, in 1912, it was incorporated under the name 'Duncan.'

You cross the Cowichan River just before you enter Duncan. To reach the Native Heritage Centre, turn left onto Cowichan Way immediately after the bridge and go to 100 Cowichan Way. The centre features visiting artists throughout the year. You might see knitting, weaving, carving or

### Cowichan Sweaters

*When the explorers first met the Natives of the Cowichan area, they were impressed with their creative skills. These artisans skilfully made blankets from a combination of reeds, dog hair, cedar bark, mountain-goat wool, duck down and 'cotton' from fireweed. They were called Chilkat blankets and were worn by First Nations leaders. The explorers took samples back to Europe, where these blankets became extremely popular.*

*The early settlers began teaching these talented Natives to knit, using sheep wool and the Fair-Isle patterns of Scotland. Cowichan sweaters today are made from naturally coloured wool that still retains the original lanolin oil, making them rain resistant. They combine the Fair-Isle patterns with Native motifs and are just as popular today as those traditional blankets were centuries ago.*

## Totem Poles

One totem pole might show the history of a family through the pictures carved on it while another may depict the ancestors of the family or its legends. Some poles also show the wealth or social standing of the family. When a chief dies, a special totem is carved to mark his grave and to depict the significant features of his life and the major events.

While totem poles were being carved for centuries before the arrival of the Europeans, carving became easier after the 1860s and the greater availability of metal tools. Some of the older poles still standing, dating back to the 1840s, are in the Kitwancool, Kispiox and Gitwangak region of northern BC.

Redcedar is the most popular wood for several reasons, including its ease of carving, its natural resistance to rotting and the large size of redcedar trees. Depending on the size of the pole, one or several carvers may work on it. The largest totem in the world is in front of the Ocean Point Resort in the Inner Harbour in Victoria. It was carved for the 1994 Commonwealth Games and stands 56 metres (184 feet) tall.

The most popular colours used on totems are red, blue and black, though yellow and white have been used to a lesser degree.

Totems carved these days combine the traditional with the modern, showing new influences in Native lives.

beading, depending on what the visiting artist specializes in on the day that you are there. As well, the centre includes a theatre, a gallery, a cafe and a restaurant with Native foods. If you want to buy a Cowichan sweater, you can get one here.

There are many craft shops in Duncan that also display various Native works.

Duncan is known as the 'the City of Totems' because of the Native totem poles along the highway and in the downtown area, close to 60 in total. This display of totems began in 1985 when it was decided to celebrate the Native heritage by erecting totem poles carved by local artists. Follow the yellow footsteps painted on the sidewalks if you want to see all of the 'totem gallery.'

If you want to see what is claimed to be the world's largest hockey stick, get back onto Highway 1 and continue northwards through Duncan. You pass Trunk Road and then Coronation Road, where the tourist information booth is. Take the next left, onto James Street and look for the community centre on the right in about one block. You can see the large hockey stick and puck on the wall of the centre. Duncan beat out many other bidders to get this memento of Expo '86 after the fair ended.

If you would like to fish the Cowichan River or hike the Cowichan River Footpath, from the community centre, return to the highway, turn right and drive back southwards to Trunk Road. Turn right (west) again and follow Trunk Road as it crosses Cowichan Way and the railway tracks. Turn left at the next traffic light.

You then cross a bridge and come to a four-way stop. Go straight ahead onto Indian Road, which curves and climbs its way past a few residences until you arrive at another four-way stop. Turn right onto Glenora Road. As you drive past the orchards here, watch for deer on the road. When you reach a Y shortly after turning onto Glenora, go right onto Vaux Road.

*Totem at Duncan*

Remain on Vaux past the Cowichan Fish and Game Association's sign for the Cowichan River Footpath and go right at the Y to continue on a gravel road. In 7.4 kilometres (4.6 miles) from the beginning of Trunk Road, you come to a parking lot on your left. Park and walk across the road into the yard with the building in it. The trail begins to the right of the building as you face it. There is a large sign that explains the history of the trail.

It is a 20-kilometre (12-mile) hike if you go all the way to Skutz Falls and it could take you five hours each way, so allow plenty of time. You are advised to wear hiking boots, have warm clothing and carry a light lunch for day hikes and carry camping gear for overnight trips.

The Cowichan River, which is 45 kilometres (28 miles) long, is one of the best fly-fishing rivers in Canada. In fact, some of it has been marked off for fly-fishing only (inquire locally). You can try for steelhead from December to April, cutthroat and rainbow in the spring and fall, and brown trout all year long.

If you are interested in birds, you can look for the three hundred different species that have been observed along the Cowichan River.

### LAKE COWICHAN VIA HIGHWAY 18

This book describes two ways to get from Duncan to the village of Lake Cowichan. (Note that the village is called 'Lake Cowichan' and the lake, 'Cowichan Lake.') Take Highway 18 for a route that is on pavement the whole way (except for

*In an effort to preserve some public land along the Cowichan River, the Cowichan Fish and Game Association obtained permission from the BC government and MacMillan Bloedel Ltd. to build a footpath on their lands along the river. They began cutting the trail through the forest by hand in 1962.*

*This trail begins at the Fish and Game Range and Clubhouse and goes along the south side of the river as far as Skutz Falls, where a suspension bridge was constructed across the river canyon. That suspension bridge has since been replaced by a forest service truck bridge. This bridge is the first crossing to the north side of the river since the start of the trail.*

*In 1969, a second phase of the trail was completed, from Skutz Falls to the Old Lake Cowichan Road. In the 1970s, two government grants enabled the hiring of people to upgrade the entire path. The trail passes through old-growth forests, beside canyons walls and along river beaches.*

*However, most of the land on the north side of the river has become privately owned and logging has destroyed much of the trail. Therefore, the trail beyond Skutz Falls, on the north side of the river, is no longer maintained by the fish and game association.*

a side trip). If you are feeling more adventurous, you can go via Riverbottom Road, a route that takes you over rough gravel roads much of the way (described later). And, if you prefer, you can skip ahead to Chapter 5 and continue northwards up the island instead.

As you head northwards out of Duncan on the Island Highway, you come to the BC Forest Museum on the right in 3.7 kilometres (2.3 miles). It is marked by a sign and an old steam locomotive on the side of the highway. The museum began as a private venture by Gerry Wellburn but the provincial government has since taken it over. It is called 'Man in the Forest.' There are over 40 hectares (100 acres) of indoor and outdoor displays that show what it was like in the early logging days and explain today's logging methods.

Climb to the top of the BC Forest Service fire lookout, see how paper is made or visit a blacksmith. A trip on the 0.9-metre (3-foot) wide narrow gauge railway takes you past a logging camp and working sawmill, over Somenos Lake on a trestle and past a number of displays around the park.

The museum is open from the beginning of April to mid-October, but the train runs only from the beginning of May to the beginning of September.

Continue northwards on Highway 1 until you reach the traffic lights at the junction with Highway 18. Turn left onto Highway 18.

For a side trip and hike to a cairn that commemorates World Wars I and II, turn right off

*Cairn, Mount Prevost*

*View from Mount Prevost*

Highway 18 in 1.3 kilometres (0.8 mile), when you reach Somenos Road. Then, in 0.7 kilometre (0.4 mile), go left onto Mount Prevost Road, which soon becomes gravel. In 3.8 kilometres (2.4 miles) there is a Y. Go left. There are logging roads off this one but stick to the main road.

In 2.2 kilometres (1.4 miles) from the Y, go left where a sign indicates parking to the left for the cairn and to the right for the lookout.

The trail to the war memorial begins to the right of the lot and goes straight up. It is a long, slow, arduous climb—sometimes over sloped rock, sometimes on a trail, sometimes on gravel. The hike could take 20–30 minutes, depending on how often you stop to rest.

At the summit, an 11-metre (36-foot) high column of granite serves as a memorial to the men of the Cowichan Valley who died during the Great World War, 1914 to 1918. A plaque was added after the Second World War to commemorate the soldiers who died in that war, 1939 to 1945. There is a wonderful view from the hill and it is worth every bit of the climb. Take it carefully coming down, though, as it is slippery in places.

In the 1930s, so many people from the same province came to settle in a certain area about 8 kilometres (5 miles) up from the base of the mountain that it became known as 'Little Saskatchewan.' Nothing of it remains today, however.

Back at Highway 18, turn right to continue towards Lake Cowichan. As you go, you are passing the Cowichan Valley Demonstration Forest, which stretches along the north side of the highway from Duncan to the village of Lake Cowichan and along the north shore of Cowichan Lake. It is a forest of young evergreens and older deciduous growth.

## LAKE COWICHAN VIA RIVERBOTTOM ROAD

Cowichan River trail start

From the highway in Duncan, turn west onto Trunk Road, which curves to the right and becomes Government Street. Stay on Government Street to Gibbins Road and turn left. Just past the turn, you pass by a hospital on your right. When you reach a Y, keep left to continue on Barnjum Road, which is gravel and is not in good shape (but any vehicle could make it if driven carefully). About 7 kilometres (4.3 miles) from the hospital you reach a stop sign. Turn left onto Riverbottom Road, which is paved for 8 kilometres (5 miles). It is narrow and scenic as it winds its way through the trees and past meadows and farms.

You can see the Cowichan River occasionally to your left as you travel along on its north side. When the road climbs, you can see over the trees to the wide and beautiful Cowichan Valley below.

If you have had enough of gravel roads, when you reach Stoltz Road you can turn right in order to continue on Highway 18. Otherwise, after Stoltz Road you descend into the Cowichan Valley. There are tall trees blocking the river on the left but there is a lovely view of the Cowichan Valley to the right. When you reach Cowichan River Provincial Park's Marie Canyon site, you can park and hike the trails to the canyon.

One-half kilometre (0.3 mile) from the Marie Canyon parking lot there is a pull-out to your left where you can look down into Marie Canyon. Then you soon reach Cowichan River Provincial Park's Skutz Falls site. Skutz Falls Forest Service Road

Marie Canyon

*Pedway, Lake Cowichan*

goes to the left over a bridge that crosses the river and canyon. The Cowichan River Footpath (described earlier) is on the other side of the river. You can cross the bridge on the walkway and stroll along the trail if you wish. Or, you may prefer to just stand on the bridge and look way down into the canyon.

Many people fish or swim in the river but you have to work your way down into the canyon to get to the water. Skutz Falls is just upstream from the bridge. This waterfall is not a long, dramatic drop of water but more a number of leisurely cascades.

There is a camping area on the right side of Riverbottom Road near the falls. Past Mayo Road, Riverbottom Road turns right and becomes Skutz Falls Road as you head northwards towards Highway 18. The tall, moss-covered trees along the road here create twilight even on a sunny day. Turn left when you reach Highway 18.

## LAKE COWICHAN

In 6.7 kilometres (4.2 miles) from Skutz Falls Road you come to a junction. The road to the right leads to the village of Youbou and beyond (described in Chapter 2). Turn left to go to the town of Lake Cowichan.

Settlers had been coming to the area since the 1880s but it was not until 1912 that the Lake Cowichan townsite was surveyed and lots were sold. That was also the year that the Esquimalt and Nanaimo Railway (E&N) ran a branch line into the area.

Stay on South Shore Road as you drive through town. You pass Central Park on your left and then cross the Cowichan River and just past the river you round a curve and drive between two concrete walls that are left over from an abandoned railway overpass. If you park to the right just past them, you can walk on the old E&N trestle over the Cowichan River. The old bridge is made of huge timbers and smells of creosote—it will doubtless bring back memories for many people who have worked

*Rail car at Kaatza Station Museum*

on or walked over similar structures in years past. Riverside Park, on the other side of the river, has benches along the river bank if you want to sit awhile.

Continue for half a kilometre (0.3 mile) on South Shore Road to the Rail's End Pub, with its large display of toy trains. Just past the pub is Faywell Park, which contains the Kaatza Station Museum, located in the old E&N railway station. Kaatza is the

*Kaatza Station Museum at Lake Cowichan*

Coast Salish name for Cowichan Lake and it means 'big lake.' The museum offers indoor and outdoor displays, including rail cars loaded with logs and a 1928 locomotive. The local tourist information office is also here.

From Lake Cowichan, you can continue along the north shore of Cowichan Lake to Youbou and Bamfield and back along the south shore of Cowichan Lake, as described in Chapter 2. Or, if you prefer, you could skip most of Chapter 2 and pick it up just as you begin to head for Port Renfrew (described in Chapter 3).

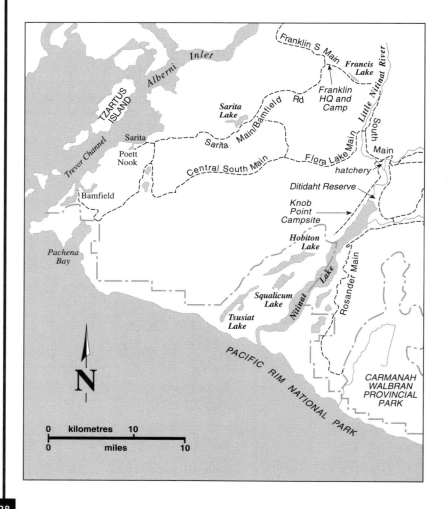

Franklin S Main

Francis Lake

Little Nitinat River

Alberni Inlet

TZARTUS ISLAND

Sarita Lake

Main/Bamfield Rd

Franklin HQ and Camp

South Main

Trevor Channel

Sarita

Poett Nook

Sarita Main

Flora Lake Main

Main

Central South Main

hatchery

Bamfield

Ditidaht Reserve

Knob Point Campsite

Pachena Bay

Hobiton Lake

Nitinat Lake

Rosander Main

Squalicum Lake

Tsusiat Lake

PACIFIC RIM NATIONAL PARK

CARMANAH WALBRAN PROVINCIAL PARK

N

| 0 | kilometres | 10 |
| 0 | miles | 10 |

# YOUBOU to
# HARRIS CREEK MAIN

*This trip is almost entirely on gravel logging roads. Fortunately, the roads are in good shape and any roadworthy vehicle can travel them, but the going is often slow. You will drive around one of the largest lakes on Vancouver Island, visit an endpoint of the famous West Coast Trail and see some of the largest Sitka spruce trees in the world.*

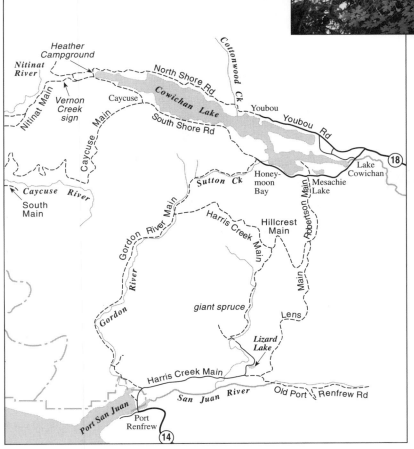

## YOUBOU & COWICHAN LAKE

To get to Youbou to start this route, take Highway 18 westbound from the Island Highway just north of Duncan and then go right onto Youbou Road instead of left for the village of Lake Cowichan. Youbou is on the northern shore of Cowichan Lake, 15.0 kilometres (9.3 miles) from the turn-off. If you are starting from Lake Cowichan, head northwards to cross the Cowichan River and turn left to follow North Shore Road and Meade Creek Road. Then make another left onto Youbou Road.

Depending on which book you read, Youbou (pronounced as if there was no second 'u') got its name from two early lumbermen, Young and Blount, or from the manager and president of the local mill, Yount and Bouten. As you drive through the village, which is in a little bay, Cowichan Lake is to your left. Although big, the lake is narrow enough that you can see the other side.

At 40 kilometres (25 miles) long and an average of 1.6 kilometres (1 mile) wide, Cowichan Lake is one of the largest lakes on Vancouver Island. It has about 102 kilometres (63 miles) of shoreline. There is good fishing here for landlocked coho salmon, steelhead, trout and kokanee.

*West Coast Trail sign*

Just follow the highway through Youbou and you pass the marina, a restaurant, chalets and a service station—note that there are no more services available along your route until you reach Bamfield. The farther you drive, the smaller and older the houses get. As you leave town, you can see the Youbou Mill on the waterfront.

After Youbou you are on a gravel forest service road as you head for the western end of the lake. Along the way, you pass some residences on the lakeshore and several recreation sites. You cross a number of bridges that span creeks that flow into the lake. You can occasionally catch sight of the lake through the trees. As you drive these logging roads, remember to watch for logging trucks with their long loads.

Starting at kilometre 15 (mile 9.3), look for gnarled old trees beside the road. Some are covered in moss and might seem as if they could be from a horror movie. They are so totally different from the trees that you are probably used to that you could almost believe that monsters are going to jump out from behind them at any moment.

You reach the end of Cowichan Lake at kilometre 19 (mile 12) from Youbou. At kilometre 19.7 (mile 12.2), you come to an intersection with four roads to choose from. Turn left. Just after your turn you pass Heather Campground, which is not one of the free forest recreation sites.

At kilometre 20.5 (mile 12.7), you reach a T intersection. Turn right onto Nitinat Main to go to Bamfield.

A little piece of historical information: the first non-Native explorers arrived in this area from Cowichan Bay back in 1857.

## THE NITINAT RIVER & FRANKLIN CAMP

Two kilometres (1.2 miles) from the T intersection, you reach a Y. Go left on Nitinat Main, following the sign for Bamfield. Another sign warns you that logging roads can be dangerous and tells you how to drive them—it also shows a map of the area.

As you near Vernon Creek, a sign at kilometre 4.5 (mile 2.8) describes the Vernon Creek Trestle Bridge, a logging bridge that was constructed across the creek in 1933 by the Industrial Timber Mills of Youbou. It was about 24 metres (80 feet) above the water and cost $3600 to build, $1400 of which was used to pay the crew of ten who built it.

After several more bridges, the road divides and you are on a one-lane, one-way road. For a short distance you do not have to worry about meeting oncoming logging trucks. Then you are back into two-way traffic.

At kilometre 18.8 (mile 11.7) you reach another T intersection, where you turn right to cross the Nitinat River and continue on towards Bamfield. (For Carmanah Walbran Provincial Park, described later, you would go left instead.)

In 2.5 kilometres (1.6 miles) from the T intersection, a road to the left, Nitinat Main, leads past the Nitinat Hatchery, located near the confluence of the Nitinat and Little Nitinat rivers. If you want to do some wilderness camping, go fishing or go canoeing, continue down the road past the hatchery for 8.3 kilometres (5.2 miles) to the Knob Point campsite on the west side of Nitinat Lake, keeping straight ahead where side roads lead up to the right. Note that the road has been deactivated by the logging companies and is in

### Tips For Driving on Gravel Roads

- *Always drive with your headlights on so that you can be seen.*
- *Cover your headlights with plastic protectors, put wire mesh in front of your radiator to prevent rock damage and mount a bug deflector to deflect bugs (as well as some of the flying rock) from your windshield.*
- *Reduce speed when meeting oncoming vehicles or passing parked vehicles and people to cut down on dust and flying rock.*
- *Put rock guards on anything that you are pulling behind your vehicle, such as a trailer or boat.*
- *Carry a tube of instant glue, such as 'Crazy Glue.' Whenever a rock chips your windshield, apply a little glue to prevent cracks from spreading.*

*Pachena Bay, Bamfield*

poor shape. However, the campsite remains popular with windsurfers, canoeists and others seeking a quiet place to camp.

Continue along South Main as it follows the Little Nitinat River and in 6.5 kilometres (4.0 miles) from the turn to the hatchery, you reach a junction. If you want to take a shortcut to Bamfield, turn left here onto Flora Lake Main, go left again on Central South Main, and then left onto Bamfield Road. However, Flora Lake Main is an active logging road, so check for signposts to make sure that vehicles are allowed on it before going that way.

To take the longer route to Bamfield, which goes past the Franklin Headquarters and Camp (where you can stop and pick up a forestry map of the area if you need one), follow South Main to the right. Although the road is partly paved, the patchy pavement is only one lane wide and logging trucks have priority to use it.

You are in the Little Nitinat River Valley, with canyon walls on both sides, as you drive the 8.3 kilometres (5.2 miles) to Francis Lake, which is on the right. The lake is usually quiet and calm and so you can enjoy the reflections in its waters. You pass the end of Francis Lake at kilometre 11 (mile 6.8) and then, at kilometre 12.6

*Suspension Bridge, Bamfield*

(mile 7.8), you reach an equipment yard with logging trailers and buildings—the Franklin Headquarters and Camp. When the gate is open, you can drive into their yard and out the other side; otherwise, take the bypass road to the left of the gate.

If you are here during working hours, stop in at the office just past the equipment yard and pick up a map of the logging roads. While you are here, ask about the road conditions and logging situations for the places that you plan to visit in the area.

When you leave the parking lot, turn right. If you want to go to the city of Port Alberni, go straight ahead. Otherwise, follow the sign that points left for Bamfield.

Back on gravel, you are on the Sarita Main, also known as the Bamfield Road. Besides the logging trucks, there is a lot of local traffic. Ignore the roads that branch off this one and in a little while you can see Sarita Lake to your right. The turn-off into Sarita Lake Recreation Site is at kilometre 14.6 (mile 9.1) from the Franklin Headquarters. If you have a small boat and want to do some fishing on a quiet lake, this is the one. If you decide to camp, however, do be aware that water levels can rise quickly during heavy rains.

*Bamfield*

You come to a stop sign at kilometre 28 (mile 17.4). A right turn here would take you to the old logging camp at Sarita and a resort at Poett Nook. From either location you can enjoy the view across Numukamis Bay to Tzartus Island. Also, there is a boat launch, and you can choose to stay at either of two campgrounds, one north of Sarita and one at Poett Nook.

Turn left to go to Bamfield and in 13.5 kilometres (8.3 miles) from the stop sign, the road curves to the right. Straight ahead, a short road leads to the beginning of the world famous West Coast Trail, which terminates to the southeast at Port Renfrew. A large sign on the left reads, 'Trail Information and Registration.' To reach the registration building, drive to the parking area at the end of the road.

From the building, you cross a small yard to reach the beach on Pachena Bay. It is a lovely place to begin your hike. Even if you are not hiking the West Coast Trail, come here just to see the sand and the ocean.

The West Coast Trail is open from May 1 to September 30. It is a beautiful but demanding 77-kilometre (48-mile) hike to be undertaken only with proper preparation and equipment. Nevertheless, the trail is so popular that Pacific Rim National Park instituted a reservations system to preserve the wilderness qualities of this

## The Life -Saving Trail

*As early as the 1600s, when this area was first being explored by the Spanish, navigators on those early ships dreaded sailing along the southwestern coast of Vancouver Island. The English explorers, who arrived in the 1700s, also soon learned the dangers of this coast: Landmarks were often quickly hidden by storms or fog, strong winds and currents often pulled ships off course and there were many rocky outcroppings on which they might founder. The entrance to Juan de Fuca Strait is only 21 kilometres (13 miles) wide and so many ships had trouble finding the 'hole' between the rocky shore of Vancouver Island on one side and the Olympic Peninsula on the other.*

*Between 1867 and 1906, there were 56 shipwrecks in the strait, with the loss of 711 lives. Of these ships, the 17 that went down in the 66-kilometre (41-mile) section between Port Renfrew and Bamfield accounted for 399 of those deaths. This area became known as one of the most dangerous shipping routes in the world and was called 'the Graveyard of the Pacific.'*

*In 1907, 'the Life-Saving Trail' was built along this section of coast, so that shipwreck survivors would at least be able to walk out to Port Renfrew, Bamfield or one of the lighthouses, instead of being stranded on some rocky shore. Rescuers on shore could also use the trail to go to the assistance of ships that they saw wash up.*

*When the number of maritime accidents was reduced, because of better navigation technology, the trail was abandoned and it was taken over by the forest. In 1969, however, the BC government rebuilt the trail for the enjoyment of hikers. It is now part of Pacific Rim National Park and has become famous as 'the West Coast Trail.'*

week-long hike. Only 52 people are allowed to begin the hike each day.

Reservations are taken beginning March 1. Within a few days, many of the best starting days in summer are taken, so book early (phone 1-800-663-6000). If you did not reserve ahead, you may still be able to hike, because there are usually some cancellations. (See Chapter 3 for more about the other end of the trail.)

## BAMFIELD

Carrying on along the road into Bamfield, you cross a bridge with a walkway over the Pachena River. Look to the right to see the old suspension bridge that was used by travellers many years ago. It is a surviving example of how the early settlers crossed these rivers before the roads came through.

Five kilometres (3.1 kilometres) from the road to the trailhead for the West Coast Trail, you reach a four-way stop in the hamlet of Bamfield, which is located on Trevor Channel in Barkley Sound.

Bamfield was named was for William Eddy Banfield, a former carpenter on a navy ship who was discharged in 1849 and came here to settle. Somehow an 'm' was substituted for the 'n' and the mistake has never been corrected.

When you arrive in Bamfield, you are actually in Bamfield East, separated from Bamfield West—the other half of the village—by Bamfield Inlet. Although the inlet is 4 kilometres (2.5 miles) long, it is only about 250 metres (800 feet) wide. But there is no bridge, so you need to take a water taxi if you want to visit Bamfield West. It is not a problem for the residents, however, since nearly everyone travels by boat. Even

**Early Cable Communication** *We take today's satellite links for granted, but long-distance communication was not always so easy. On September 19, 1902, the cable ship Colonia began laying a trans-Pacific communications cable from Bamfield to Fanning Island, a tiny coral island in the middle of the Pacific, near the equator. This cable transmitted only one message at a time, by Morse code key, at a speed of just eight words per minute. Each time a message arrived, the operator at the receiving end of the trans-Pacific cable would then re-key it onwards via other cables to its eventual destination.*

*This communication system lasted until 1959, when a connecting cable was run to Port Alberni and the Bamfield station closed. The new link to Port Alberni had 80 voice channels. The ex-station building now houses the Bamfield Marine Station, a marine biology research centre jointly operated by three universities based in British Columbia and two from Alberta.*

the children, instead of taking a bus to school, take a school boat. It is not surprising that Bamfield has been nicknamed 'the Venice of Vancouver Island.'

You can see many of the local boats, including the school boat, from the 2 kilometre (1.2 mile) boardwalk that stretches between two government wharves on the shore of Bamfield West. There is a Coast Guard rescue service stationed here, to aid sailors in distress out on the Pacific Ocean. And, even though there is now a road to Port Alberni, the *MV Lady Rose* still arrives from there three times a week with supplies, mail and passengers (see Chapter 6).

Across Trevor Channel from Bamfield there are a number of islands that you can explore by canoe or kayak. If you are here early in the spring, join the whale watchers who come to see the thousands of gray whales that pass through Barkley Sound on their way northwards to their summer feeding grounds.

# Carmanah Walbran Provincial Park & Cowichan Lake's South Shore

## CARMANAH WALBRAN PROVINCIAL PARK

Head back, either via Franklin Camp or via the short cut, to the junction of Nitinat Main and South Main, just before where you first crossed the Nitinat River. Turn right onto South Main to go to Carmanah Walbran Provincial Park. Since the Carmanah parking lot is about 35 kilometres (22 miles) from this junction, check to see if you need gas or supplies. If so, you can turn right at kilometre 5.7 (mile 3.5) to stop in at the Ditidaht Native Reserve, your last chance to stock up.

As you continue on South Main beyond the turn-off for the reserve, you are following the southeastern shore of Nitinat Lake, which is actually an inlet connected to the ocean at Whyac and thus has both tides and salty water. Nitinat, Hobiton and Tsusiat lakes together form 'the Nitinat Triangle,' a great wilderness canoeing route for well-prepared, experienced paddlers.

*Hikers bound for West Coast Trail*

Nitinat Lake is said to have the best windsurfing conditions in Canada or the United States and so you might see windsurfers out on the lake. Bring your board along if windsurfing is your sport too.

Then you turn east, away from the lake, and follow up the Caycuse River until the road crosses it. Just after the bridge, turn right onto Rosander Main, which turns back along Nitinat Lake. It soon climbs above the lake and continues southwards. After a number of twists and turns, you arrive at the main parking lot for Carmanah Walbran Provincial Park.

Carmanah Walbran Provincial Park exists to protect a magnificent ancient forest. One of the people who fought to save these trees from logging was the late Randy Stoltmann. He first hiked in the Carmanah Valley in 1982. At that time, logging was scheduled to begin in 2003. When Stoltmann returned in 1988, he discovered that the planned logging date had been moved forward fifteen years and the company was already building roads. He got support from the Western Canada Wilderness Committee, the Sierra Club and the public and together they were able to get MacMillan Bloedel to stop building roads until an assessment could be done.

Word of one particular spruce, now known as 'the Carmanah Giant,' had first begun circulating in 1956, but no one had been able to confirm its existence. Finally, in 1988, the story was proved to be true; it was found 1 kilometre (0.6 mile) from the ocean. At 95 metres (312 feet) tall, it is thought to be the world's tallest Sitka spruce.

Initially, MacMillan Bloedel proposed to protect only 99 hectares (245 acres). However, in the spring of 1990 the BC government dedicated 3592 hectares (8876 acres) of the lower valley as parkland. In 1994, after continuing efforts by environmentalists and the public, land in the upper valley was added, as was part of the adjacent Walbran Valley.

In recognition of Stoltmann's part in popularizing the Carmanah Valley and in securing its eventual protection, a memorial was erected in his honour and 'Heaven Grove' was renamed after him.

While a trail to the Carmanah Giant built by the Western Canada Wilderness Committee in 1988 has been closed by BC Parks, allegedly because of its deteriorating condition, there are several other wonderful trails to take. The park's Sitka spruce groves, believed to be some of the tallest in the world, contain more than 230 of these big trees that stand over 70 metres (230 feet) tall and have trunks 3–4 metres (10–13 feet) in diameter.

## CAYCUSE & HONEYMOON BAY

After enjoying Carmanah Walbran, return to Cowichan Lake via Rosander Main, South Main and Nitinat Main. There is a boat launch here where you reach the lake.

Turn right onto South Shore Road to follow the lakeshore eastwards. Keep going straight at kilometre 7.0 (mile 4.3) from the boat launch, where Caycuse Main leads off to the right and there is a sign for the settlement of Caycuse. Farther on you come to a few houses.

At kilometre 10.5 (mile 6.5), look to your left to see the Caycuse Sort on the lakeshore. Logs are brought here from where the logging is happening

*View from Youbou Lookout*

and piled in stacks. The logs are then sorted according to size and type and quality of wood before being loaded onto trucks or made into booms for transportation to the sawmill, pulpmill or other destination. Caycuse is believed to be the longest-operating logging camp in North America.

Pull over and walk to the edge of the cliff on the left at kilometre 20.3 (mile 12.6). You are at Youbou Lookout, so named because you have a perfect view of Cowichan Lake with Youbou and the hills on the other side. You might see a boat pulling a log boom on the lake. Look towards the left to see the valley of Cottonwood Creek running through the hills.

Three kilometres (1.9 miles) from Youbou Lookout you come to Honeymoon Bay Lookout, from which you can get a lovely view of the lake.

If it seems a little warmer along the southern part of the lake, it is because the south arm of the lake acts as a heat trap. The area has an average maximum temperature of 24 degrees Celsius (75 degrees Fahrenheit) during the summer—one of the highest in Canada.

In 4.7 kilometres (2.9 miles) from Youbou Lookout, the road splits. Ahead is the Gordon River Main logging road, which goes southwards towards Port Renfrew (it is not as good as the Harris Creek Main described later in this chapter).

Instead follow the road that curves to the left. It becomes paved and just 0.4 kilometre (0.2 mile) down the pavement, look for a narrow side road to the Wildflower Reserve on your right. There is no sign along the main road but if you look to the right when you reach the narrow road you can see one in the trees.

Turn off here, drive in and park in the small lot. (If you have a motorhome or are pulling a trailer, the nearest parking is 0.8 kilometre (0.5 mile) down the road at Honeymoon Bay, but it is worth the walk.) A large sign lists wildflowers and shows their pictures. Some of the 23 different wildflowers that you can look for are cow-parsnip, small-flowered buttercup, vanilla-leaf, pink fawn lily, two-leaved false lily-of-the-valley and enchanter's nightshade. Vancouver Island's largest known growth of pink Easter lilies is found here. Spring is the time to find trillium and pink erythronium in bloom.

The sign says this ecological reserve is part of a world system of natural areas set aside for scientific research and education, so please leave the flowers alone. Take along only photographs, sketches and memories.

Drive through Honeymoon Bay and cross Sutton Creek. There are two stories about how Honeymoon Bay received its name. One is that it was so named when a man, Henry March, brought his bride out here to homestead. The other is that it was named when a man travelled back east with the purpose of marrying and then bringing his bride out here. However, he never returned.

Just down the road from Honeymoon Bay you cross Robertson River and then you arrive at the settlement of Mesachie Lake.

## MESACHIE LAKE

As you drive into the settlement of Mesachie Lake, there is a flashing light. Continue through the light and go one-third kilometre (0.2 mile) to Forestry Road and turn left. It is less than 1 kilometre (about 0.5 mile) to the office of the BC Forest (Cowichan Lake) Research Station.

The office is open from 8 AM to 4 PM, Monday to Friday, except on holidays. Guided tours are not offered, but the staff will give you a map that you can use as a guide for walking the grounds. Two of the points of interest along the trails are a second-growth forest of Douglas-fir that began growing in 1911 after a fire in 1909 and a stand of red alder, a tree that (with the help of bacteria living in its roots) takes nitrogen from the air and puts it into the soil, unlike most kinds of trees, which take nitrogen from the soil as a nutrient.

The staff have been studying trees—such as the Douglas-fir, western redcedar, Sitka spruce, western hemlock and yellow-cedar—since 1929.

*Harris Creek Canyon*

In the village of Mesachie Lake, look for the 33 different species of trees that were brought here from around the world by a Mr. Stone, the local sawmill owner and the founder of the settlement, during the 1940s. You can see 240 examples of these exotic trees lining South Shore Road and along other streets.

Continue reading if you wish to go on to Port Renfrew by logging roads. If you would prefer to go to Duncan and the Island Highway instead, continue towards Lake Cowichan, which is only a few minutes' drive away. From there you can take Highway 18 to Duncan.

From the flashing light in Mesachie Lake, turn southwards and you are headed to Port Renfrew, initially on Robertson Main. Go left at the Y at kilometre 2.9 (mile 1.8). You are now on Hillcrest Main, a gravel logging road. There are a few bridges to cross and hairpin curves to slow down for, but for the most part it is easy to follow. You can see Lens Lake to your right at kilometre 17.5 (mile 10.9) from the flashing light.

At kilometre 21.2 (mile 13.1) you reach a T intersection. Turn left to get onto Harris Creek Main (posted as a 'public route') and follow Harris Creek downstream.

Watch for the small blue-and-white sign for the 'The Harris Creek Spruce Tree' at kilometre 27.3 (mile 17.0). Pull off the road as far as you can to the left and park. Walk along the short trail through the bush. Just past a sign that tells you about the plants and wildflowers in the area, you cross a little bridge and reach the giant tree.

There is a fence that surrounds and protects the tree. A path leads all the way around it so that you can look at it from all sides. The Harris Creek Spruce is really massive, really tall—it has a diameter of 3.4 metres (11.1 feet) and measures 82 metres (269 feet) to its top. You can look up but you will not be able to see the top.

*Harris Creek Canyon*

You cross a one-lane bridge over Harris Creek at kilometre 32.1 (mile 19.9) from Mesachie Lake. Look to your left to see the Harris Creek Canyon. There is a pull-out just after the bridge where you can stop if you wish to walk back onto the bridge for a better look at the canyon.

Just past the bridge you reach pavement, but it is broken up and interspersed with gravel for the next while. You pass Lizard Lake and a recreation site to your left. The shore of this small lake is a nice place to have a picnic.

Keep right at kilometre 38.4 (mile 23.9), where a road joins this one from your left. The road to the left, the Old Port Renfrew Road, goes northeastwards towards Shawnigan Lake. Check that it is passable, because in 1984 a logging company blocked off the bridge across Williams Creek because of its bad condition. Also, parts of the road are recommended only for four-wheel drive vehicles.

Thirteen kilometres (8 miles) from where the Old Port Renfrew Road joined, there is a major road, Deering Road, to the left. Turn left onto it to go to Port Renfrew. (Straight ahead is Gordon River Main, which leads back to Cowichan Lake.)

Just after the left turn off Harris Creek Main, you cross a long one-lane bridge. Soon the road splits—keep right—and then the two branches rejoin. In 2.4 kilometres (1.5 miles) from the left turn you cross another long one-lane bridge, this one over the San Juan River.

Half a kilometre (0.3 mile) more brings you to a stop sign at the western end of Highway 14—and the town of Port Renfrew. See Chapter 3 for more on the area.

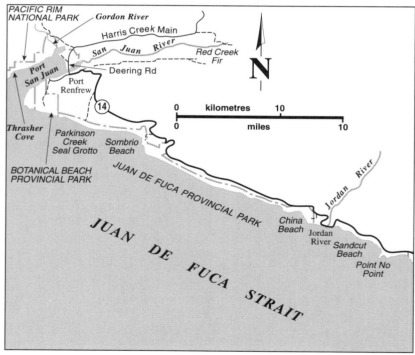

# PORT RENFREW to COLWOOD

For most of this route you will be on Highway 14, which follows along Juan de Fuca Strait. Although you will not be driving close beside the water until you reach Jordan River, you will have many magnificent views from the road above the strait.

Between the road and the strait is the Juan de Fuca Marine Trail, which you can hike from Port Renfrew to China Beach or in reverse. If you would rather just walk parts of it, there are several access points where side roads lead down to it, as it passes through the trees or runs alongside a beach.

Travel Highway 14 with caution, because even though it is paved, it has sharp curves, narrow bridges and steep descents.

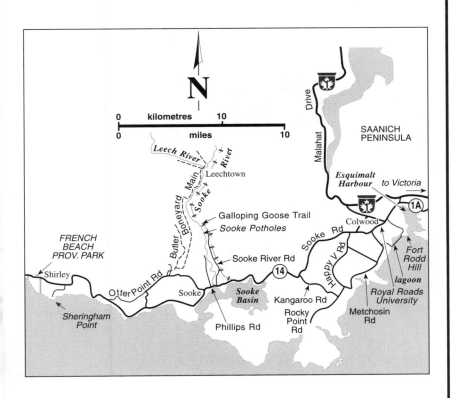

# PORT RENFREW & AREA

If you came down Harris Creek Main and turned left onto Deering Road (as described in Chapter 2), you cross over the San Juan River on the long one-lane bridge, and then reach the junction with Highway 14 in Port Renfrew. A left turn here immediately puts you onto the highway to Jordan River, Colwood and Victoria—but it is worth spending some time exploring the Port Renfrew area.

Port Renfrew is at the southeastern end of the world-famous West Coast Trail (described more fully in Chapter 2), which has Bamfield at the other end. Straight across the highway at this junction is the parking lot for the registration building for hikers starting at this end. To reach the actual trailhead by vehicle, return along Deering Road for 1.5 kilometres (0.9 mile) and turn left. You drive through the Pacheenaht Indian Reserve before you reach the Gordon River. For a fee, a boat will ferry you across.

Because the first 5 kilometres (3 miles) of the trail at this end are the worst part, many hikers bypass it by taking a Trailhead Charters boat from the government wharf in Port Renfrew across Port San Juan to join the trail at Thrasher Cove. The company also offers trips from the wharf to the trailhead on the west side of the Gordon River, in case you want to hike the whole trail (phone 250-647-5468 for more information.)

If you wish to explore the tide pools at Botanical Beach, from the junction with Highway 14, turn right (west) and drive past the general store. Where the road curves to the right, you can visit the tourist information booth, which is on the left at that curve. Drive to the sign that reads 'Botanical Beach' and turn left.

*West Coast Trail Registration, Port Renfrew*

As you follow the rough and narrow gravel road, you can see Juan de Fuca Strait to your right. When you reach the provincial park boundary, the road improves a little. Go to the second parking lot to get to the Botanical Beach trailhead.

The trail is mainly downhill but is not steep. Be careful, however, because it is made of pieces of shale that can sometimes slide under your feet. After about a 15-minute walk, you reach a small picnic area and steps down to the beach. It is nice to sit here and listen to the sound of the waves coming in.

If the tide is out, go exploring—but do take into account the fast tide changes, which could trap you on a little island of higher rock that is quickly disappearing under the sea.

*Botanical Beach*

Over the centuries, the waves lapping against the rock have carved the shore into caves, pools and basins. Each pool or basin is like an aquarium when the tide goes out because within the water it retains are marine organisms such as sea urchins, jellyfish, starfish and abalone. You can see other rock of a different material exposed where the covering layer has been worn away. Please treat all the creatures with respect and leave everything as you found it when you leave.

Botanical Beach was the site of the world's first marine research centre, constructed in 1901, and was later a gun emplacement during the Second World War. Now it is part of a provincial wilderness park and nature reserve.

At the other end of the picnic area is the trailhead for the 49-kilometre (30-mile) long Juan de Fuca Marine Trail. The trail ends at China Beach and could take three or four days to complete. There are other access points along the highway to Victoria, such as Parkinson Seal Grotto Provincial Park and Sombrio Beach, if you want to hike only part of the trail.

If you plan to hike this trail, there is a notice at Botanical Beach that you should read before heading out. It tells about the weather, beach accesses and trail conditions. A sign explains about the construction of the trail.

From the junction at the end of Highway 14 in Port Renfrew, head eastwards along the highway towards Jordan River and Victoria. In 2.2 kilometres (1.4 miles), the highway curves to the right. There is a gravel road to the left and one straight ahead. If you want to see a giant Douglas-fir tree, 'the Red Creek Fir,' make the sharp turn onto the gravel road to your left.

This one-lane road is full of potholes. In some places it is falling away and there have been rockslides on it. It used to be a main logging road but it is now

*Botanical Beach*

closed beyond the fir tree and is not maintained as much as it used to be. However, it is well used and even a motorhome could make it to the parking lot; if you are pulling a trailer, though, you should leave it at the highway.

You can occasionally see the San Juan River as you follow it upstream. At kilometre 2 (mile 1.2) you cross Falls Creek. Falls Creek Trail, one of several signposted hiking trails off this road, is just after that bridge.

You sometimes travel between trees whose branches meet overhead. At kilometre 11 (mile 6.8), there is a Y. Go to your left. Just past the Y you come out of the trees and have a great view of the valley below to your left and the mountains on the other side.

*Botanical Beach*

Kilometre 12.3 (mile 7.6) brings you to a small parking lot. Park here and continue down the road on foot. It is almost grown over and just when you think that you are going to run out of road, there is a sign that points to the trail going to the right and into the trees.

This part of the 10–15-minute trail is pretty rugged: you clamber over dead trees, roots and shale, as well as crossing streams on logs or rocks. You can actually see the fir before you reach it, as it stands alone against the blue sky.

According to a plaque nearby, the Red Creek Fir has a circumference of 12.6 metres (41 feet, 2 inches) and a height of 74 metres (241 feet). Look up at the crown; it has a 23-metre (75-foot) spread. This Douglas-fir is estimated to be between 700 and 1000 years old.

## THREE STOPS ON
## THE JUAN DE FUCA MARINE TRAIL

Continue along the highway and in 3.8 kilometres (2.4 miles) from the road to the fir is the road to Parkinson Creek Seal Grotto Provincial Park, another place to get access to the Juan de Fuca Marine Trail.

*Juan de Fuca Park*

Turn right off the highway onto the gravel road, which is in poor condition. When you reach the Y, go right. As you work your way down to the parking lot, you have a great view of the strait. At kilometre 3.7 (mile 2.3) from the highway, you reach the parking lot. From the trailhead here you can take the trail to the left towards Sombrio Beach or to the right towards Botanical Beach.

In the spring, harbour seals congregate to give birth to their young in the cave or grotto from which the park gets its name. The cave is not readily accessible, however, and visiting it is not encouraged, so as to avoid disturbing the seals.

As you continue along Highway 14 towards Jordan River, there are a number of pull-outs from which you can enjoy more views of the strait and the snowcapped Olympic Mountains across the strait in Washington.

It may interest you to know that 'Juan de Fuca' is the oldest European name in the province. A Greek named Apostolos Valerianos, who was hired by Spain to find another ocean that connected with the Atlantic Ocean, used Juan de Fuca as a pseudonym. In 1592, he sailed into the strait that separates what are now Washington State and Vancouver Island and it was named in his honour.

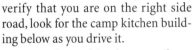

**A Historical Perspective** *Take a moment to consider what was happening in European history around the time that the Red Creek Fir was sprouting from its seed, 35 to 50 generations ago on a human scale:*

*Around 1000 AD, the Vikings sailed to North America. They started a settlement at what we now know as L'Anse-aux-Meadows in northern Newfoundland, which many scholars believe to be Leif Ericson's Vinland. Then, in 1066, Normans from France conquered England.*

*The first of the four Crusades by the Christians to reclaim the Holy Land from the Muslims took place between 1096 and 1099. (The fourth and last Crusade took place from 1201 to 1204.)*

*The first stories of King Arthur and the Knights of the Round Table were started in 1100. They were modelled after a historical figure named Arthur, who had by that time been dead for five hundred years.*

*Robin Hood, a hero to the common people, is said to have lived during the late 1100s and early 1200s.*

*The Magna Carta, a document that put the English king under the law and took away many of his powers, was signed by King John in 1215.*

*When we view the situation in this way, we get a whole new appreciation of the lifespan of a majestic tree such as the Red Creek Fir.*

At kilometre 9.6 (mile 6) from the Parkinson Creek road there is a gravel side road that makes a sharp turn to the right off the highway and winds its way down to Sombrio Beach. If you want to verify that you are on the right side road, look for the camp kitchen building below as you drive it.

From the parking lot, start down the trail until you come to a Y. To the left, the Juan de Fuca Trail continues to China Beach; to the right, to Botanical Beach. If you want to go to Sombrio Beach, take the path to the right. Then, when you come to a suspension bridge, one of the 30 bridges on the trail, take the narrow trail to the left just before it.

*Hiking the Juan de Fuca trail*

Sombrio Beach is lovely, with lots of sand and huge driftwood logs. The only sound is the waves crashing against the shore, a call to surfers.

Back on the highway, continue eastwards to China Beach Provincial Park and the end of the Juan de Fuca Marine Trail. It is a park for picnicking and hiking, but you probably would not want to swim here unless you enjoy cold water. As you sit on the beach, keep a watch for passing whales.

## JORDAN RIVER

About 3.5 kilometres (2.1 miles) from the road to China Beach, you curve to the right and come down a hill towards the village of Jordan River. Look to your left as you descend to see a log-sorting area. Then you are right down along the ocean at Jordan River, with its few houses and a cafe.

You cross the river from which the village got its name near where it enters the ocean. There is uncertainty as to whether the Jordan River itself was named after a family who settled here in 1862 or whether Spaniards named it for Alejandro Jordan, a chaplain who visited Vancouver Island in 1790.

It is not at all obvious from here that the Jordan River is used to produce electricity. In 1911, a 26,400-kilowatt hydroelectric generating plant was built about 7 kilometres (4.5 miles) upstream. Then the power output was boosted to 150,000 kilowatts in 1971, at that time providing most of the power needed for the southern part of Vancouver Island.

On the right, just beyond the Jordan River, you can pull in at the Jordan River Recreation Area. If you like to birdwatch and are here between October and December, watch for black-legged kittiwakes along the tide-rip near the river mouth. During the summer, this beach is a nice place to picnic and watch the waves lap up onto the shore. In winter, however, the waves can be 2–3 metres (6–10 feet) high, which makes the area popular with surfers—the West Coast Surfing Association has even built cabins here.

*Sombrio Beach*

*Sheringham Point cliffs*

## SANDCUT BEACH, POINT NO POINT & SHIRLEY

In 3.7 kilometres (2.3 miles) from the bridge over the Jordan River, there is an unmarked parking lot on the right side of the highway. A wide, well-maintained trail takes you through a deep, dark forest. Level at first, it soon begins to descend. There are boardwalks, steps, tree roots and bridges to help you on your way down to Sandcut Beach. As you approach, you can hear the surf through the trees.

The beach is thickly covered with rounded stones and has lots of driftwood. It is a relaxing, secluded place to watch the rolling surf.

Continue along the highway to enter the District of Shirley and reach Point No Point. Stop in at the tea house here or walk down to the bottom of the cliffs to the little cove.

The explanation of how this feature was named is quite simple: When early navigators came from the east, they saw an unmistakable headland. But when they came from the west, there was no point to be seen. So, it became known as 'Point No Point.' In 1895, a survey officially designated it as 'Glacier Point.' However, the residents liked the original name better and in 1957 they successfully appealed to have 'Point No Point' made the official name.

A short distance past Point No Point you reach the entrance to French Beach Provincial Park, where you can camp. Walk down to the beach here in the spring or fall and you will have a good chance of seeing migrating gray whales. If you are short on supplies, the French Beach Mini Mart is located on the highway just past the park entrance.

In 2.9 kilometres (1.8 miles) from the French Beach Provincial Park, look for Sheringham Point Road on the right; it is marked by a large sign for a cafe. If you would like to go look at the Sheringham Point Lighthouse, turn right onto this road. Then take the middle road when you reach a three-way branch. When you see a sign at kilometre 1.7 (mile 1.1) from the highway that warns you that you will not be able to turn around beyond this point, park and continue on foot.

It is only a short distance until you come to a locked gate, but you can see the lighthouse through the chain-link fence. For a better view, and the best place to take pictures of the lighthouse, take the path alongside the fence, which leads to cliffs overlooking the strait. (The cliffs are too steep for you to go down to the water, however.)

When the lighthouse was constructed in 1907, it guided ships along the Juan de Fuca Strait lit by an oil lamp that shone through a Fresnel lens. In 1925, a foghorn powered by compressed air was added. Both the light and the foghorn are now automated and the lighthouse is closed to the public.

When you get back to the junction at the highway, look to your right to see the Shirley Community Hall, built in 1937, and Shirley Pioneer Park. Established in 1885, Shirley was named by the area's first postmaster, after his home in England.

## SOOKE & LEECHTOWN

This area was visited by Manuel Quimper in 1792 and put under Spanish rule. He traded with the Natives from his ship but did not establish a settlement. Six years later, Britain took the area over. A small mountain north of Sooke Basin was named after Quimper.

*Moss Cottage, Sooke*

Quimper also explored across the strait, around present-day Neah Bay. As a result, the second Spanish post on the northwest coast was established there.

As you come into the town of Sooke, one block after you pass Tomminy Road on the left, you reach Maple Avenue. Just to your right on the corner of Maple and the highway is a cairn honouring the landing of the first settler, Captain Walter Colquhoun Grant. He moved here in 1849 and built a water-powered sawmill, the second one in the province. If you continued down Maple, you would arrive at the government wharf on Sooke Harbour, Canada's most southerly harbour.

The route to Leechtown, the site of Vancouver Island's one and only gold rush, is via active logging roads that are not signposted. If you want to see that part of British Columbia's history—or if you are looking for a place to camp for the night—turn left

Sheringham Point Lighthouse

onto Otter Point Road, which is just a few blocks east of Maple Avenue. In 5.0 kilometres (3.1 miles) you reach Young Lake Road. Turn right and in one-half kilometre (0.3 mile), turn right again, onto Butler Road (which becomes Butler Main further along). You know that you have made the proper turn if you come to gravel after a further half kilometre (0.3 mile).

In 1.2 kilometres (0.7 miles) from the beginning of Butler, you reach Boneyard Road (or Boneyard Main). Turn right onto it and follow it for 12.7 kilometres (7.9 miles), until you reach a narrow road to the right. This short track leads past a campground and up to the shore of the Sooke River. The site of Leechtown is across the river and if the river is low, you can wade across and look for the remnants of this historic town.

If you would prefer to hike or cycle into Leechtown, take the Galloping Goose Trail, which is on an abandoned railway bed that leads past the site. (See p.51.)

Near here, 16 kilometres (10 miles) up the Sooke River from where it flows into the ocean, is where it is joined by the Leech River. It was at this confluence, in July of 1864, that Peter Leech and members of a government exploration team discovered gold. Almost immediately, the area was swarming with prospectors. Leechtown sprang up so quickly that most of its stores, hotels and saloons were made of canvas.

By the following spring, one hundred thousand dollars in gold had been taken from the river banks, but the supply was soon gone and so were the miners. The only buildings left were the gold commissioner's log house and a few cabins.

Back on the highway, continue through Sooke. When you are almost at the bridge over the Sooke River, turn left onto Phillips Road. Pull over just off the highway to visit the Sooke Museum. At the entrance into the museum yard there is a mountain-ash, which the Scots know as the rowan-tree. A sign reads:

## Captain Walter Colquhoun Grant

In 1849, Walter Grant became the first independent settler on Vancouver Island. He had signed a contract with the Hudson's Bay Company agreeing to pay one pound sterling for every 0.4 hectare (1 acre) of land that he wished to purchase. Part of the contract was that he would enlist the services of two couples or five men from England for every 40 hectares (100 acres) that he bought.

His farm was less than 40 hectares (100 acres) in size but he nevertheless had seven men working for him clearing the land and putting in a crop. However, when some of his men left for the California gold-fields, he soon followed. He eventually returned to England.

Grant is responsible for introducing the yellow-flowered Scotch broom that grows so well on the southern part of the island. On a winter trip to Hawaii (then known as the Sandwich Islands), he was given some broom seeds by the British consul there. When he came back, he planted the seeds at Sooke. They thrived in the temperate climate and have come to be a dominant feature in many places. While broom is pretty to look at, plant biologists and ecologists worry about the consequences of how effectively it has been displacing native vegetation.

*Popular in this area with its early Scottish settlers was the Rowan-tree. According to Gaelic folklore the Rowan is the guardian, the protecting power, the tree of life.*

*Conversely, if harmed or disrespected, the Rowan-tree was thought to be infinitely malignant. It was said that the Rowan could be used to impart a curse on one's enemies.*

The oldest standing building in Sooke is also here on the museum grounds. It is the Moss Cottage, built in 1870. Its evocative name comes not from its appearance, however. Instead, the owners, James and Mary Ellen Welsh, named their home in memory of Mary Ellen's mother, who was born into the Moss family.

## THE GALLOPING GOOSE & THE SOOKE POTHOLES

Return to the highway, turn left and cross the Sooke River. To head for the Sooke Potholes (no, the name does not commemorate a really bad piece of road!), get into the left lane and turn left onto Sooke River Road.

Just after you turn the corner, you pass Fred Milne Park. Then, 2.4 kilometres (1.5 miles) from the highway, there is a parking lot on your right that provides access to Galloping Goose Regional Park.

Galloping Goose Regional Park is nearly 60 kilometres (40 miles) long but only 30 metres (100 feet) wide. The reason for the park's existence is a trail that follows an old rail bed. Very popular with cyclists, horseback riders and hikers, it is Canada's first 'rails-to-trails' conversion.

The railway, a part of the Canadian National Railway, went from Victoria through View Royal, Colwood and Metchosin to the Sooke Basin and up the Sooke River to Leechtown. This rail line got its name from the railway's

**The Lost Tunnel** *One autumn evening in the late 1950s, a prospector named Ed Mullard was on his way back to his camp after an unsuccessful hunting trip near the former site of Leechtown. As the light was fading, he came across an oblong hole that had been cut into the rock at the base of a cliff. There were seven steps down, which he followed, and he arrived at an archway carved into the rock. Though he had only matches to light his way, he went through the archway and entered a gallery about 3 metres (10 feet) long and over 1.8 metres (6 feet) high.*

*He walked across this room and at the far end, to his right, he found another archway. From here it was seven more steps down to another gallery. In this second gallery, he found water. Although he saw a third archway leading still farther into the rock, he turned back.*

*Mullard never returned to the cave, nor did he tell of its whereabouts. Rumour has it that the Spanish hid bars of gold in a cave in the area in the 1700s, although no one has found the tunnel or the gold to verify it.*

*Galloping Goose trail sign*

**The Rowan-tree** *Folklore has it that in centuries past, throughout northern Europe, twigs from the rowan-tree were used to guard against sorcery and its branches were hung around farmyards to shield the inhabitants from evil. Rowan-trees were planted to protect against the powers of darkness and travellers who had to spend a night on the road tried to find a rowan-tree to sleep under as a defence from the terrors of the night. And those were just some of the many uses of the rowan-tree, the most magical plant in the woods. According to an old Scottish ballad, it was so popular that the witches cried—because they had no power wherever a rowan-tree was planted.*

*The rowan-tree, commonly known as the European mountain-ash, is native to northern Europe. It is a member of the rose family and is therefore related to apples and hawthorns. Both the rowan-tree and native mountain-ashes are found throughout Canada and the northern United States.*

*Settlers brought the tree over as a familiar, and protective, reminder of home, but they did not just depend on it for protection. They picked the berries for jelly, used the bark for dyeing and tanning and shaped the small branches into hoops for barrels.*

*Today this hearty tree is loved for the beauty of its bright red berries in late summer and its lovely yellow and scarlet leaves in the fall.*

Gas Car #15813, which was nicknamed 'the Galloping Goose.' Its front part was a shortened version of a steam locomotive and the rear part, which looked like a trolley, had seats for passengers and also carried the mail.

If you followed the Galloping Goose northwards from this parking lot, you would pass the Sooke Potholes (described shortly), cross several creeks, see a number of farms and travel beside canyons and lakes. In 10 kilometres (6 miles), you would reach the old site of Leechtown, described previously. There are many other access points along the length of the trail as well. While you are hiking, watch for bald eagles and turkey vultures.

Continue along Sooke River Road and in 2.6 kilometres (1.6 miles) from the access road for the Galloping Goose, you reach the parking lot for Sooke Potholes Provincial Park. A wide trail begins at the far end of the parking lot. Just to the left of it you can go down to a small riverside beach where you can picnic or play in the water.

Follow the trail, which is really a road, as it climbs up from the river. From this main trail, other trails lead into the bush and down to beaches along the river. When you come to a gate across the trail, in about fifteen minutes, you have come to the end of the park. While the land beyond the gate is private property, many people do go around it. About fifteen minutes more along the trail would bring you

*Sooke Potholes*

*Sooke Potholes*

to a huge, partially completed building on the left.

The story is that this building was the dream of a businessman who wanted to build a luxurious resort here overlooking the Sooke River, where meetings and conventions could be held in a tranquil setting. He began work in the early 1980s, using big timbers for supports and rock for the walls and for a huge fireplace. Then he ran out of money in the middle of construction and everything was halted. Eventually, he was able to get more financing to complete it to the stage that it is at now, but then his funds ran out again. Over time the building has begun to deteriorate.

Unfortunately, the best vantage point from which to see the Sooke Potholes is from this building. If you do decide to continue past the gate to investigate this building, walk through it carefully, at your own risk. Watch for holes and weak areas in the floors. Go to the edge of the cliff and the walkway and follow it to the lookouts. Below are the canyon, the Sooke River and the potholes.

The water of the Sooke River moves slowly in the summer and there are small pools—the potholes—all along it. These potholes were formed when the rushing waters of the spring run-off swirled trapped boulders against the softer bedrock of the river bottom. Notice how the water flows over the edge of one pool into another and then into another. If you went farther along the road, you would come to a path down to these pools. You can go swimming in them or dangle your feet in the water or just lie on the rocks and sunbathe.

## The Metchosin Flitch

*During the early 1900s, the divorce rate in Victoria was said to be the highest in Canada. In an effort to reduce the rate, the Farmers' Institute at Metchosin decided to revive an old English custom—it began presenting an annual award called 'the Metchosin Flitch.'*

*'The Flitch,' a side of pork that had been salted and cured into bacon, was given to the couple who could most truthfully state and honestly prove that they had not had a fight in the past 366 days.*

*The practice was discontinued in the 1930s. Unfortunately, there is no record if this award helped lower the divorce rate during the years it was awarded.*

# METCHOSIN & COLWOOD

Continue along Highway 14, known here as 'Sooke Road,' heading towards Victoria. In 7.0 kilometres (4.3 miles) from the Sooke River Road, you pass 17 Mile House, a large two-storey building on the left side of the highway. It was built in 1900 and was a stage stop on the road from Victoria to Sooke. If you wish to stop for a visit, it is now a pub.

**Colwood** *What we now call Colwood used to be the Hudson's Bay Company's Esquimalt Farm. Edward Langford, one of the company's employees, and his family, were moved to the farm in 1851. Langford was the one who changed the name to 'Colwood,' after his family home in Sussex, England.*

*Langford liked to party and he held several picnics and dances at the company's expense. In one year alone he drew 320 litres (70 imperial gallons or 84 US gallons) of liquor from the company store. He also lived beyond his means and was constantly borrowing money from his employers, sometimes as much as eight times the amount of his annual salary. When the Hudson's Bay Company decided to terminate his services, he fought back, even suing the company. However, he eventually admitted defeat and returned to England in 1861.*

*The neighbouring community of Langford was named after him.*

You enter the community of Metchosin and at kilometre 2.4 (mile 1.5) from 17 Mile House, turn right off the highway onto Kangaroo Road. In 5 kilometres (3.1 miles) from its beginning, you reach a stop sign at Rocky Point Road. Turn left. At the following stop sign, turn right onto Happy Valley Road. Then turn left onto Metchosin Road when you reach the next stop sign.

As you continue along Metchosin Road, you enter the community of Colwood. Look to your right to see Victoria across the harbour. When you reach Lagoon Road, turn right. It curves a bit and then you come to a stop sign. Straight ahead there is a parking area next to the ocean. Turn left onto Ocean Boulevard. You can park along the right side of the boulevard if you want to enjoy a stroll on the shore.

While the ocean is on your right, the Esquimalt Lagoon, the largest lagoon on southern Vancouver Island, is on your left. It is believed to have been formed during the last ice age when a block of ice broke from a receding glacier and melted in the depression it had formed.

The lagoon is a federal bird sanctuary where black brant geese, swans and herons— as well as many other different species of waterfowl—come for the winter.

Across the lagoon you can see Royal Roads University. On the grounds are the Royal Roads Botanical Gardens. These were once part of the Hatley Park Estate, which was owned by James Dunsmuir, a wealthy former premier and lieutenant-governor of BC. He built his home, Hatley Castle, on his 280-hectare (700-acre) estate. Upon his death the federal government took it over and established Royal Roads Military College. In 1995 it became a civilian institution and was renamed 'Royal Roads University.' (For more on James Dunsmuir and his father, Robert, see the middle of Chapter 5.)

If you want to get a closer look at Hatley Castle, one way to get there is to stay on Sooke Road instead of turning onto Kangaroo Road back in Metchosin. (Or you can turn left once you reach Highway 1A at the end of this chapter and then go left onto Highway 14.) Turn in at 2005 Sooke Road, where there is a large sign. While there is a small charge for parking, you can wander through the botanical gardens for free.

Several years ago, the castle's ballroom was used to film a large ball scene in a movie. In the process, the floors were ruined. Unfortunately, the building has been closed to the public ever since.

Look to the right, near the entrance to Esquimalt Harbour to see Fisgard Lighthouse, which is on an islet of the same name. While the red-topped white lighthouse looks small from here, it is actually 14.3 metres (47 feet) tall and on clear nights its light can be seen 16 kilometres (10 miles) out to sea. You get the best view as you cross the bridge over the entrance to Esquimalt Lagoon.

**Hatley Park** *James Dunsmuir spent a good sum of his profits from his coal, shipping and lumbering businesses on his Hatley Park Estate, overlooking the entrance to Esquimalt Harbour. He allocated large areas for Italian and Japanese gardens for the enjoyment of his guests. He had trails for those who liked to ride horses and paths for those who chose to walk, as well as tennis courts, fish ponds and guesthouses. It took almost one hundred staff members to look after the grounds.*

*Inside his castle, which was completed in 1908, were guest rooms, a ballroom for the many dances that he held, a library, a large kitchen and a huge dining room. The estate was the focal point of the social season for Victoria's upper class.*

In 2.6 kilometres (1.6 miles) from where you turned onto Ocean Boulevard, you come to the entrance to Fort Rodd Hill National Historic Park and Fisgard Lighthouse National Historic Site. Hours are 10 AM to 3 PM every day.

Fort Rodd Hill was constructed in 1895 to defend the naval base at Constance Cove, on the opposite shore of Esquimalt Harbour. In its over fifty years of service, the fort never fired a shot in anger. It was active up until 1956, when more sophisticated weaponry made it obsolete. The fort was turned into a National Historic Park in 1962.

From the park, walk out along the causeway to the Fisgard Lighthouse. The lighthouse was built in 1860, using bricks that had served as ballast on ships coming around Cape Horn. It is the oldest lighthouse on the west coast of Canada. While the lighthouse itself is not open to the public, there are displays to see in the former keeper's house.

When you leave the parking lot, turn right. Then follow Ocean Boulevard to Highway 1A. Turn right and then you can either stay on Highway 1A or get onto Highway 1 if you want to go to Victoria. The area north of Victoria, the Saanich Peninsula, is described in Chapter 4. If you would prefer to head up-island instead, take Highway 1 northbound when you meet it.

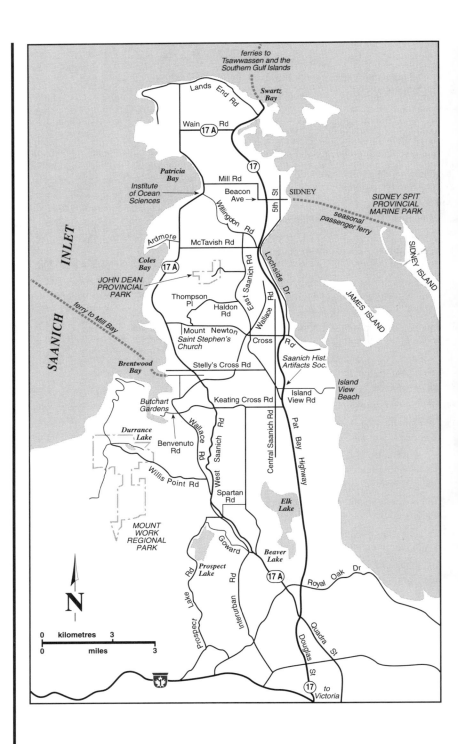

# THE SAANICH PENINSULA AND THE SOUTHERN GULF ISLANDS

The Saanich Peninsula is a very beautiful, but small, part of Vancouver Island. The area north of Victoria is mostly pastures, crops, hayland, woodlands and animals.

Many people think that only Saltspring, Saturna, Mayne, North and South Pender and Galiano islands are true Gulf Islands. Others claim that these islands named above are just the main Southern Gulf Islands and that all islands in the Strait of Georgia as far north as and including Gabriola Island are part of the larger group. Still others say that if an island is anywhere in the Strait of Georgia, it is a Gulf Island. But why waste time arguing when you can be out enjoying them?

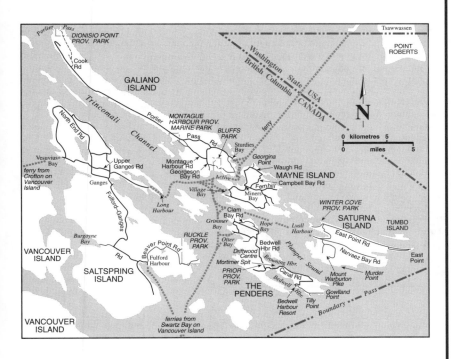

# The Saanich Peninsula

Highway 17, also known as the Pat (Patricia) Bay Highway, is congested and fast, with little to see. Highway 17A, the West Saanich Road, is more relaxing, pastoral and scenic. Either will take you to the ferry at Swartz Bay.

The Saanich Peninsula includes Victoria, Sidney and the municipalities of Oak Bay, Esquimalt, Saanich, Central Saanich and North Saanich.

## THE SAANICH PENINSULA via HIGHWAY 17A

As you go northwards on West Saanich Road, you will have regional parks, grain farms, dairy farms, rows of corn, orchards, market gardens, herb farms, tree farms, greenhouses and stables to see as you drive through the countryside. Every spring, the South Vancouver Island Direct Farm Marketing Association puts out a list of about forty farms where you can buy fresh fruits and vegetables, and even artesian well water. You can get a list from any member farm.

To begin your northward trip, from downtown Victoria, head northwards on Blanshard Street until it curves left, joins Douglas Street and then becomes an expressway (Highway 17). Take the first exit, north/westbound on West Saanich Road. Watch out for horses and cyclists as you drive.

The beginning of West Saanich Road takes you through quiet farmland and trees. Just past where Old West Saanich Road comes in from the right, you reach Goward Road. You can turn left here if you want to go to Prospect Lake Road, which leads past Prospect Lake. While there is a park where you can picnic at each end of this small lake surrounded by hills, swimming in the water is not recommended because of the high coliform counts.

### Settlement on the Island

With the Americans moving farther westwards into Oregon and the lack of a well-defined boundary for Oregon Country, the Hudson's Bay Company decided to explore northwards from its Fort Vancouver (now Vancouver, Washington) near the mouth of the Columbia River in order to establish headquarters on solidly British land. The company surveyed the southern tip of Vancouver Island in 1842 and in 1843 Fort Victoria was built. This outpost became the first non-Native settlement on Vancouver Island.

When the 49th Parallel was agreed upon as the boundary between the territory belonging to the United States and British holdings in 1846, Fort Vancouver was way south of the line. It was abandoned by the company. Victoria then became the headquarters for British trade on the West Coast.

In 1849, in order to keep the area under Britain's control, Vancouver Island was made a crown colony under the direction of the Hudson's Bay Company.

Most of the early British communities on Vancouver Island were begun because of the discovery of coal. When the demand for coal declined, some of these towns died while others found different industries to keep them going.

*Butchart Gardens sign*

At kilometre 4.5 (mile 2.8), just north of the Dominion Astrophysical Observatory, you reach a junction with Spartan Road to the right and Prospect Lake Road to the left (an alternative point for quick access to Prospect Lake). Prospect Lake Market Garden, on the left at the junction, has been in business since 1913 and sells fresh fruit and vegetables throughout the summer.

Continue along West Saanich Road until kilometre 6.8 (mile 4.2) from the beginning, where you can turn off to go to Mount Work Regional Park. If you wish to do so, go left onto Wallace Drive, then left again onto Willis Point Road. Follow this road until you reach the park.

Within Work Park is Durrance Lake. While the lake is relatively small and camping is not permitted, there are some beautiful hiking trails through a tall forest of redcedar, hemlock and Douglas-fir. Other trees include alder, arbutus and maple— together they keep the area in twilight. The trails are best for experienced hikers, so do not venture too far if you are still a novice. Also note that fog can cover the area quite quickly, making it harder to find your way.

Drive northwards again on West Saanich Road for 3.6 kilometres (2.2 miles) and you reach a junction where Keating Cross Road is to the right and Benvenuto Road is to the left. (*Note:* the word 'cross' is abbreviated with an 'X' on some signs.) Turn left onto Benvenuto if you want to go to the famous

*Butchart Gardens*

*Butchart Gardens*

Buchart Gardens. As you drive the 1.8 kilometres (1.1 miles) to the gardens, you may be surprised to see double-decker tour buses. Brought to the Victoria area to support its British image, they can be quite impressive if you have not spent time in Victoria or been to England.

When you arrive at Butchart Gardens, take a long, relaxing stroll through the Japanese, Italian, Rose and Sunken gardens on the 20 hectares (50 acres) of land (moderate entrance fees). See the begonias, perennials and lawns and visit the greenhouse and gift shop. The gardens open at 9 AM daily year-round, but evening closing varies depending on the time of year. If you are there in the evening, stay until dark, when the lights create a magical atmosphere.

Jenny and Robert Buchart arrived on Vancouver Island in 1904. Robert built a cement manufacturing plant that used limestone from their property and Jenny began planting flowers around their home. When the limestone quarry near their house was depleted, Jenny began to turn the eyesore into a sunken flower garden. She had dirt brought in and spread on the bottom. She arranged to be lowered over the edge in a chair so that she could direct the work. When the preparatory work was done, she established an Italian garden.

Every time the couple travelled abroad, they would bring back plant clippings for their gardens and by the 1920s it had become a tourist attraction. The gardens are now run by their grandson.

Continue northwards on West Saanich Road. At Brentwood Bay, expect to find congestion and heavy traffic. Follow the signs for the Brentwood/Mill Bay ferry to the dock, where it is quieter and you can look out over the bay while enjoying an ice-cream cone, a picnic lunch or a cup of coffee. This ferry provides a short-cut across

Saanich Inlet, between the northern part of the Saanich Peninsula and places north of the Malahat.

Once you are through the town and headed northwards once again on West Saanich Road, the quiet countryside returns. In 4.4 kilometres (2.7 miles) from Benvenuto Road you reach Mount Newton Cross Road. Turn right onto this road, which is more like a country lane. To visit one of the oldest churches in BC on its original site and in which services have been held continuously since its construction, watch for St. Stephen's Road on the right at kilometre 0.7 (mile 0.4). Turn onto it and go past the newer church to the old St. Stephen's Anglican Church, built in 1862 (see photo, page 62). The doorway into the church is flanked by two huge, tall trees, which must have been planted when they and the church were young.

A sign at the church reads:

*If you are weary, come in and rest.*
*If you are sad, come in and pray.*
*If you are lonely, come in and make friends.*

There is an adjoining cemetery where you may wish to look at the names and dates on the headstones.

Return to Mount Newton Cross Road and turn right. In 1.7 kilometres (1.1 miles) from St. Stephen's Road, you come to Saanichton's school—the fields nearby are a good place to see skylarks. As you approach Saanichton, watch out for pedestrians and for hidden driveways.

The village of Saanichton is at the centre of an agriculture area. Millions of daffodils are shipped from the region every spring, some as far away as Florida. On the Labour Day long weekend, the village holds the province's oldest surviving agricultural fair, which had its beginnings in 1871.

Go through the first four-way stop to the second one, at East Saanich Road, and on the left-hand corner is the Prairie Inn Hotel, which used to be the Prairie Inn Store (see photo, page 63). This building was built in 1893 to replace one constructed here in 1859, the Prairie Tavern. Today's establishment also contains a cottage brewery.

There are two museums in Saanichton. To get to the Pioneer Log Cabin, turn left onto East Saanich Road to find it about 100 metres (300 feet) along on your right. It will give you an idea of what life was like in the days of the pioneers.

**Skylarks** *If you are a birdwatcher, as you drive through the Saanich Peninsula, watch for Eurasian skylarks. They were brought here in the early 1900s by English settlers who were homesick for something familiar. The hundred pairs of birds liked the Saanich area and slowly increased in numbers. The Saanich Peninsula is the only place in North America where they have been successfully introduced. They are attracted by the daffodil and vegetable farms, where they like to feed on insects and build their nests. However, their numbers are now dwindling because urban expansion has been reducing their habitat.*

*The skylark is slightly bigger than a sparrow and is streaked with brown. Its song of trills and warbles stands out from those of other birds in total length, clarity and the great heights from which it is often sung.*

*St. Stephen's Church*

To explore the grounds of the Saanich Historical Artifacts Society, turn right onto East Saanich Road and drive south for 2.8 kilometres (1.7 miles) to Island View Road. Turn left, cross the highway and then immediately go left again onto Lochside and follow it to the grounds. Here you can see restored and working farm equipment, including an 1882 threshing machine and a 1907 horse-drawn steam engine that used to power a sawmill. On leaving, if you want to visit Island View Beach, continue along Island View Road.

It is about 3.2 kilometres (2 miles) from the grounds to the beach. The road is flat for the first 2 kilometres (1.2 miles) and then you begin climbing a gradual hill. Take in the view of the ocean before you descend to the beach, which offers over 6 kilometres (4 miles) of shoreline to explore. The campground here is believed to be the only one on the Saanich Peninsula with showers, so get here early if you plan to spend the night.

Take East Saanich Road or the Pat Bay Highway back to Mount Newton Cross Road and continue northwards on East Saanich Road. If you want to take a side trip through a lovely valley, turn left onto Haldon Road. Drive slowly to enjoy the beauty. When the road curves to the left and becomes Thompson Road, follow it back southwards to Mount Newton Cross Road. Here a right would take you back to West Saanich Road and then another right there would take you farther northwards along the peninsula. If you prefer, turn left onto Mount Newton Cross Road and then left again onto East Saanich Road to make a loop.

Keep on going along East Saanich Road for 1.3 kilometres (0.8 miles) past Haldon Road until you reach Dean Park Road, where you can turn left if you want to do some hiking in John Dean Provincial Park. Take the trail to the summit of Mount Newton for a great view that includes Mount Baker, across the Strait of Georgia in Washington State. There are also a number of other trails to choose from throughout the park's 174 hectares (430 acres). The land for this park (established on December 9, 1921) was the first land ever donated to the provincial parks system.

From Dean Park Road, drive 1.2 kilometres (0.7 miles) farther up East Saanich Road to McTavish Road. From here it is only a few minutes' drive to the town of Sidney. Turn right onto McTavish and either cross the highway and follow Lochside Drive and Fifth Street northwards into town, or take Highway 17A northwards to Beacon Avenue and turn right. Go to the eastern end of Beacon Avenue to reach Bandstand Park, where you can listen to a performance starting at 2 PM each Sunday during the summer. There is a different type of music each week.

If you want to spend some time on a nearby island, you can take a passenger-only ferry from the dock at the end of Beacon Avenue to Sidney Spit Provincial Park on Sidney Island.

*Prairie Inn, Saanichton*

Sidney Island was known as Mutcha to the Native people who used it as a summer home. The legend goes that Mutcha was a giant rat who, as a punishment for its greed, was turned into the island by the spirit god Swaneset. The spit is said to be Mutcha's tail.

Go to Sidney Island for a day of hiking or carry your tents and supplies with you to spend the night. It is a popular spot and camping is by reservation only; call 1-800-689-9025 to reserve a campsite. This island is also a popular destination for kayakers and canoeists. So is Princess Margaret Marine Park, which encompasses all of Portland Island and is located about halfway between Swartz Bay and Saltspring Island.

Return to McTavish Road and head westwards. Then turn right to go northwards when you get back to West Saanich Road.

To visit Coles Bay Regional Park, turn left onto Ardmore Drive just north of McTavish Road. Follow Ardmore to Inverness, turn left and park in the lot at the end of the road. It is a short hike to the secluded bay, where you can picnic or enjoy the sun on the beach.

At kilometre 2.4 (mile 1.5) from McTavish is the entrance to the Institute of Ocean Sciences, Patricia Bay branch. This branch is one of nine across Canada that study the oceans that surround our country on three sides. Researchers at this facility also monitor selected bodies of fresh water as far east as the Manitoba border. Within the institute's 28,000-square-metre (301,400-square-foot) building are machine shops, a water tunnel, laboratories, a library, an acoustic test tank and a high-pressure test facility.

Tours of the Ocean Sciences Institute are offered Mondays and Wednesdays at 11 AM and they last about one and one-half hours. Since the tours are very popular, it is best to book ahead—the number to call for reservations is 250-363-6518.

West Saanich Road then follows the shore of Patricia Bay, which was named after the daughter of the Duke of Connaught, who was governor general when the two of them visited the area in 1912.

Continue along West Saanich Road, past Wain Road, to Lands End Road and turn right. Follow this road to the junction with Highway 17 and then turn left towards Swartz Bay, where you can catch a ferry for the Southern Gulf Islands or for the mainland. Along the way there are viewpoints from which you can see several of the Gulf Islands. Many of the homes along this road have English names and some are styled after English cottages.

## HIGHWAY 17

If you are in a hurry to get from Victoria to the ferries at Swartz Bay, take Highway 17 instead of Highway 17A, a trip of about 31 kilometres (19 miles).

Should you wish to visit just one or a few of the places mentioned in the preceding write-up of the route via West Saanich Road, you can get to many of them by turning off the highway at the nearest major crossroad.

If you are somewhat curious about the machinery outside at the Saanich Historical Artifacts Society grounds, you can see some of it from Highway 17, on the right shortly after you pass Island View Road.

Continuing northwards on Highway 17, you can see a marina to your right as you near Swartz Bay and the ferry terminal for the Gulf Islands.

Plan to be at the ferry dock at least one-half hour before the scheduled departure time. Weekdays are the best time to travel and, if possible, avoid holiday long weekends, when you might have to wait a ferry. While you are waiting, consider that BC Ferries manages to transport over eight million vehicles per year throughout its system.

# The Southern Gulf Islands

The Strait of Georgia separates Vancouver Island from the mainland. It is about 200 kilometres (125 miles) long and varies from 29 to 48 kilometres (18 to 30 miles) in width. The northern end of the strait is marked by the Discovery Group of islands near Campbell River. The southern end is marked by the Gulf Islands.

The Gulf Islands are part of a small, narrow region that lies in the rain-shadow of the mountains on Vancouver Island. This physiographic area is part of the Georgia Depression and in biogeoclimatic terms, it approximately coincides with the Coastal Douglas-fir Zone. The climate is drier than for adjacent areas, with cooler summers and warmer winters.

For thousands of years, the nomadic Coastal Salish Natives of the area hunted, fished and gathered plants on the islands. However, with the coming of the Europeans, these traditional patterns began to change dramatically.

In 1791, a Spanish lieutenant named Francisco Eliza was so captivated by the strait and all its islands that he called it El Gran Canal de Nuestra Senora del Rosario del Marinera, which means 'the Great Channel of Our Lady of the Rosary of the Seafarers.' When Captain George Vancouver arrived in 1792, he renamed it after his patron, King George III. But, thinking that he was sailing in a gulf, he called it 'the Gulf of Georgia.' Although Captain Vancouver and his crew found their way out of the 'gulf' by heading north and thereby circumnavigating what is now Vancouver Island, it was not until 1865 that the mistake was officially corrected, when Captain George Henry Richards surveyed the waters and recognized the Gulf of Georgia to be a strait. Its name was changed to 'the Strait of Georgia' but the islands remained 'the Gulf Islands.'

In the late 1800s and early 1900s, travel between the islands was by rowboat, canoe or sailboat. None had docks for large ships. On the islands, travel was mainly by foot. None of the islands had a hospital. In 1905, the Anglican Church's Columbia Coast Mission set up floating hospitals that travelled to communities and logging camps to administer to the sick and injured. Even now, only Saltspring Island has a full-service hospital.

Today, the smaller, less-populated or unoccupied islands in the strait can still be reached only by private boat or by water taxi. Saltspring, the Penders, Saturna, Mayne and Galiano islands have car-ferry service from Vancouver Island, from the mainland and between themselves. But the Southern Gulf Island ferry schedule is such that it is not possible to visit from island to island easily if your time is limited. And, because the ferries can get quite crowded in summer, some routes, particularly those from Tsawwassen, may require advance reservations if you plan to bring your motor vehicle. (Within BC, call 1-888-223-3779; from outside, 1-250-386-3431.)

Since camping facilities range from non-existent on Saturna to a few campgrounds on the others, check the ferry schedule before beginning your tour. (As an alternative to camping, all of these islands, Saltspring in particular, have little resorts and/or bed-and-breakfast offerings.) Since ferry schedules can change from year to year, be sure that you have a current schedule (available at ferry terminals and tourist information booths) or phone for sailing times on the particular days on which you plan to travel.

Although this book is about driving backroads, you are not going to get much out of your trip to the Gulf Islands if you stay in your car and restrict your experience to what you can see through your windshield. By all means, get out and stroll along the beaches, enjoy a walk through the woods, stop in at little cafes and artists' studios and talk to the local people if you really want to find out what the Gulf Islands are all about.

While the Gulf Islands can seem like paradise, they are more fragile than you might expect. To do your part, let the beautiful wildflowers go unpicked and untrampled and, if you brought a pet, keep it on a leash or in your vehicle. Since the roads of the Gulf Islands are mostly narrow and curving, with poor visibility, please drive with extra care and be on the lookout for pedestrians, cyclists, equestrians, deer and stray livestock. If possible, take your recyclables and garbage with you off the island, because waste disposal is usually a problem for residents. Finally, because the islands are so dry in summer, do your part to conserve water and also respect bans on smoking and campfires designed to protect the tinder-dry grasslands and forest from fire.

## SATURNA ISLAND

Saturna Island is easiest to reach from Vancouver Island's Swartz Bay ferry terminal. However, once each day a ferry runs to Saturna from Tsawwassen, south of Vancouver, and from Mayne Island. Five days a week a ferry arrives from North Pender Island.

Most of the services are at the island's ferry dock at Lyall Harbour. There are no campgrounds and only a few bed-and-breakfasts. Two stores, a pub, a bakery and two galleries are located at or near the harbour.

'Saturna' comes from *Saturnina*, which was the name of the seven-gun Spanish ship that

**Murder Point** *Although it is not shown on most maps, near the southern end of Saturna Island, on Plumper Sound, there is a place known as 'Murder Point.' It received its name after Frederick Marks and his daughter were murdered here in November of 1862. The family had been moving its belongings to the island in two boats and they were separated in Plumper Sound during a storm. They had just landed when Marks was shot by Natives. His daughter ran off.*

*It was not until April of the next year that news of the murder reached Victoria. Four ships were sent to search the coastline and arrest the killers. The daughter's body was found stuffed into a crevice and covered with boulders. The ships attacked a Lamalchi Native village on Kuper Island, which is to the north, near Chemainus. Eleven men and six women were arrested and the village was wiped out. Four of the Native men were hanged in July of 1863.*

*Unfortunately, there is no record of the Natives' version of what happened.*

*Boat Passage, Saturna Island*

was used to explore the region in 1791. It is the most southeasterly of the Gulf Islands and is about 23 kilometres (14.5 miles) long and an average of 9 kilometres (5.5 miles) wide. The early settlers planted orchards, raised sheep and worked in sandstone quarries. There are now about 260 permanent residents on the island.

From the ferry, go up the main road, East Point Road. Follow it to the left past Narvaez Bay Road to a junction with Winter Cove Road. Turn left to go to Winter Cove Marine Park, a park with few amenities—a picnic site, baseball diamond and hiking trails.

If you are on the island on July 1, take in the annual Saturna Lamb Barbeque, a Dominion Day (Canada Day) tradition that attracts boaters from the Victoria area and other Gulf Islands. Begun in 1950, it was for years held at Saturna Beach. Now it takes place at Winter Cove Marine Park.

From the junction, East Point Road continues to the left to follow alongside the shore. It becomes Tumbo Channel Road when it is across the channel from Tumbo Island. At the end of Tumbo Channel Road is the East Point Lighthouse. It was built in 1888 and is on federal land, but the building and grounds are closed to the public to protect the privacy of the staff who live here. Down at the shore you can walk along the shell-and-pebble beach and watch for orcas (formerly known as 'killer whales') out in the ocean.

To visit Mount Warburton Pike, return along East Point Road to the junction with Narvaez Bay Road. Make a sharp left onto Narvaez and then a right onto Harris Road, across from Saturna General Store. Make a hairpin left onto Staples Road. Follow the long, winding gravel road through an ecological reserve towards the summit of Mount Warburton Pike. This reserve was set up to protect a small forest of coastal Douglas-fir, one of the last virgin stands of this tree in the area.

The mountain was named for an adventurous Englishman, Warburton Pike, who, after canoeing down the Yukon River in the early 1890s, came to the island and opened a stone quarry on Plumper Sound.

There is a hiking trail from the end of Staples Road that leads along the top of a ridge overlooking North and South Pender. It begins in the park but soon enters private land owned by J.M. Campbell. Ask for his permission (phone [locally] 539-2470) if you want to hike this trail.

## SALTSPRING ISLAND

Saltspring Island, also spelled 'Salt Spring,' has three ferry terminals. The ferry from Vancouver Island's Swartz Bay arrives at Fulford Harbour, on the southern end of Saltspring. Another ferry sails from Crofton (described in Chapter 5), which is north of Duncan, and makes fourteen crossing per day to Vesuvius Bay, which is towards the northern end of Saltspring. The third ferry makes a round trip from Tsawwassen to Long Harbour in the morning and again in the evening. The time taken for this last trip varies depending on whether the ferry stops in at North Pender, Mayne and/or Galiano islands.

The majority of the island's services are in Ganges, with the village of Fulford Harbour coming in a distant second. There are all types of accommodations, from luxurious resorts and bed-and-breakfasts to campgrounds and even a hostel on Saltspring.

This island is 29 kilometres (18 miles) long and about 11 kilometres (7 miles) wide and within this area it has 160 kilometres (100 miles) of roads. The largest of the Gulf Islands, it was called Chaun, 'facing the sea,' by the Natives. The first non-Native settlers called it 'Admiral Island,' but decided to change the name to reflect the fourteen salty springs found towards the northern end of the island. The springs, which are on private property, range from 1 metre (3.3 feet) to 25 metres (82 feet) in diameter. Sea blush, a plant with small pink flowers, grows on the edges of these springs.

*Vesuvius Ferry, Saltspring Island*

Saltspring was the first of the Gulf Islands to see non-Native settlement when a group of African-Americans, who had bought their freedom and had been to the Fraser River gold-fields, applied to Sir James Douglas to establish a community on the island in 1857. Over time, other settlers arrived and the African-American community disappeared, its surviving members apparently having moved elsewhere. New residents found the growing conditions good and so Saltspring, along with Mayne Island, had bountiful orchards long before the Okanagan became famous for its fruit. Today the island has over nine thousand residents, many of them artisans.

There is a lot to see and do on this island. You can hike the trails, ride horses and visit craft and art galleries. Or you can take advantage of the island's lakes and adjacent ocean to swim, fish, kayak, canoe or boat. A tour of homes on the island is offered in July. To buy tickets, complete with a map and admittance button, phone (locally) 537-2125.

When you arrive by ferry from Swartz Bay, you land at Fulford Harbour. Just west of the village, at the head of Fulford Harbour, is St. Paul's Roman Catholic Church, built between 1880 and 1885. It is a small stone building—the materials for it were brought across the treacherous Sansum Narrows from Vancouver Island by Native war canoes. The

**The Pit-lampers** *The forests of Beaver Point were a favourite area for pit-lampers, forerunners of today's spotlight poacher. They used to sneak into the woods with bicycle lamps to shine on the animals, captivating them with the light, so that they could easily shoot them.*

*One pit-lamper always boasted that he could tell what type of animal he had in the light by the colour of its eyes. One evening, while on his nocturnal hunt, he saw two sets of eyes. He quickly raised his rifle and shot both animals. Proud of his success, he went looking for his pair of horses to carry his kills home. He found his horses—right where he had shot them.*

canoes landed in Burgoyne Bay and the stones were loaded onto stone boats and pulled by oxen through the Fulford Valley to this site. (Stone boats were small platforms made of thick planks onto which a farmer would pile rocks that he wanted to remove from his fields and which were pulled by horses, oxen or a tractor.) This church is very much like the well-known 'Butter Church' of the Cowichan Valley on Vancouver Island (see Chapter 1).

If you would like to hike on trails through second-growth forests, wander along the shore or go camping, take Fulford-Ganges Road up from the ferry only a very short distance and then turn right onto Beaver Point Road. Follow the signs to Ruckle Provincial Park. The park is named after the Ruckle family, who settled on the land in 1872. The family sold it to the government one hundred years later. The park headquarters are in a log building that was constructed in 1908 for one of the men of the family and his fiancée. When the engagement was broken off, the basement of the house was used to store potatoes. The residents of the area still call the building 'the Potato House.'

As you drive along the Fulford-Ganges Road beyond the church, watch for the Salt Spring Museum on your right. It has displays of Native and non-Native history. Then look to the left for Burgoyne Bay Road. Cattle rustlers used to use Burgoyne Bay as a hiding and loading area. A favourite of the rustlers were the Texas longhorns raised by a rancher named John Maxwell. Nearby, Mount Maxwell still bears his name.

As you continue northwards, the houses begin to get more plentiful. Then you go down a hill and you find yourself amidst the hustle and bustle of downtown Ganges. Every Saturday between April and October there is a farmers' market from 9 AM to 3 PM. Go check it out at Centennial Park, right downtown on the Fulford-Ganges

Road, and you will find a wide variety of produce, baking, crafts and seafood. There is even live entertainment on some days.

Rock climbers will want to attempt 'the Wall,' situated inside a tall, thin building at 268 Fulford-Ganges Road, behind the Salt Spring Community Centre, just as you enter Ganges. Beginning to advanced climbers from along the west coast of Canada and the United States visit the site to test their skills. It is open to the public for a user fee, and there is equipment to rent, but the times vary, so you will need to check their schedule (locally, 537-9971).

From the centre of Ganges, follow first Lower Ganges Road and then Upper Ganges Road northwards. Just past Long Harbour Road on the right, turn left to stay on Upper Ganges Road (Robinson Road continues straight). After it crosses North End Road, it becomes Vesuvius Bay Road. As you enter the settlement of Vesuvius Bay and near the ferry dock, watch on your left for Langley Street. Popular Vesuvius Beach, reached by a short flight of stairs from Langley Street, is said to offer the warmest ocean swimming on the island.

## THE PENDERS

Ferries arrive at Otter Bay on North Pender four times per day from Swartz Bay and twice from Tsawwassen. There are also daily ferries from Saltspring, Saturna, Mayne and Galiano islands.

'The Penders' is actually two islands, North Pender and South Pender, which are joined by a 90 metre (300 foot) bridge. For centuries, however, the two islands were one. In the days before there were roads across the island and everyone travelled by boat, residents wanting to go from one side of the island to the other would have to drag their boats across the strip of land that separated Browning Harbour from Bedwell Harbour, or they would have to row all the way around the southern or northern end of the long island.

Then, in 1902, at the request of residents, the government dredged out the strip of land, known as Indian Portage, which was situated between the northern and southern sections. As land travel improved, residents wanted the best of both worlds and so, in 1955, the bridge was constructed.

Most of the services are on North Pender, at the Driftwood Centre, which is near the head of Browning Harbour on Bedwell

### Murder at Mortimer Spit

*Two men, who were sailing around the islands, stopped to camp at Mortimer Spit one night in 1863. They were joined by five Natives— three men and two women. The sailors shared their tea and food and spent the evening visiting with the Natives. It was dark when the two men finally retired into their tent. Suddenly the Natives began shooting into the canvas. They killed one man and wounded the other. Nevertheless, he was able to frighten them off and then went to Victoria to report the murder. The authorities arrested the three Native men and one woman. They were tried and found guilty. The men were hanged and the woman received a life sentence.*

*There is no known record of the Natives' version of this tragic sequence of events. We can only speculate as to whether the attack might have been provoked by resentment at the arrival of the outsiders on their land or if there was some other motivation.*

Harbour Road. If you are here on a Saturday, check out the farmers' market held at the centre. Just up the road, there is camping at Prior Centennial Provincial Park.

Most of the place names on the Penders come from the early settlers. For instance, Port Washington, which is on Grimmer Bay—and Grimmer Bay itself too—were named after Washington Grimmer, the first postmaster on the island. Up until 1891 he made regular trips by rowboat to Mayne Island to send out and collect the mail.

When the Europeans began to settle in the 1860s, the East Saanich Natives remained on their hunting and fishing grounds at Hay Point at the entrance to Bedwell Harbour on South Pender—though they are no longer there today.

On North Pender, early industries included a cedar roofing-shake plant, a lubricating-oil and fertilizer plant, a herring-saltery, a commercial brickyard and apple orchards. Logging was important on South Pender. The two islands together are now home to about two thousand permanent residents.

The Penders have 61 kilometres (38 miles) of shoreline and are famous among the islands for their numerous beach accesses.

On North Pender, turn left onto Otter Bay Road shortly after you come up from the ferry, and you soon arrive at Port Washington on Grimmer Bay. For a nice drive through tall cedars, maples and fir trees, take Port Washington Road from Port Washington towards Hope Bay. Then, just a short distance up the road, turn left onto Clam Bay Road. Follow it through the tall trees as it curves past Welcome Cove and ends up at Hope Bay.

Follow Bedwell Harbour Road southwards from Hope Bay as it goes past fields and sheep farms to the Driftwood Centre. If you want to lie on a sandy beach or swim in warm waters, watch for the sign for Browning Harbour Marina on your left just past the shopping centre and take the side road to Hamilton Beach.

To reach the bridge to South Pender, continue southwards, now on Canal Road, keeping left where a side road to the right goes to Magic Lake Estates. Once across the one-lane bridge from North Pender to South Pender, a road on the left leads to Mortimer Spit, a slim area of grass and sand.

On South Pender, Canal Road follows along the northeastern side of the island until it turns right and becomes Spalding Road. At this corner you could go left onto Boundary Pass Drive and then left onto Conery Crescent if you want to go down to the water at Little Bay—a site recommended for anyone seeking a nice, quiet place for a picnic.

South Pender has many coves and harbours, some of which were used as ports by rum-runners on their trips down to Seattle during US Prohibition. Today, canoeists, kayakers and other boaters with more recreational purposes in mind visit these secluded beaches.

Take Spalding Road to cross over to the southwestern shore of the island. When you reach a junction at the bottom of a steep hill, you can turn right to visit the resort and marina at Bedwell Harbour. Or head left at this junction to continue southeastwards on Gowlland Point Road. As you drive towards Gowlland Point, watch for Craddock Drive, which leads to a beach at Tilly Point. The underwater caves near here are a popular destination for scuba-divers. Carry on down the main road to explore Gowlland Point, which juts out into Boundary Pass.

## MAYNE ISLAND

The ferry sails several times per day from Swartz Bay to Village Bay on Mayne Island. There are also two ferries from Tsawwassen each day and there are two from Saltspring Island every day except Friday, when there is only one. A ferry runs daily from North Pender, Saturna and Galiano islands.

Most of the services on the island are at Miners Bay. There are no provincial parks or public camping and limited private camping, but there are lodges, two inns, bed-and-breakfasts and resorts. Mayne Island holds the oldest annual fair on the Gulf Islands on the third weekend in August, at the Agricultural Hall in Miners Bay.

After perhaps five thousand years of seeing little human activity besides seasonal Native fishing camps, Mayne Island was 'discovered' by explorers from Spain and England. In 1881, settlers on the island found a penny and a knife on Georgina Point that must have been left by a member of Captain George Vancouver's crew, the first English explorers here, when they sailed from Mayne Island in 1794.

Some people claim that Mayne Island was the first place in the province to grow apples. Although apples were never a major cash crop, Mayne is well known for its King apple. You will drive by many orchards on the island.

When you get off the ferry at Village Bay, turn left onto Village Bay Road to go to Miners Bay. This bay received its name from the miners who camped here on their way from Vancouver Island to the Fraser River gold rush in 1858. There are many historic sites in Miners Bay. At the Springwater Lodge you can eat a meal in a building that was constructed in 1890s. From it you can see Miners Bay and Active

*Georgina Point Lighthouse, Mayne Island*

Pass, with all its ferries and other ships. The museum is in the original jailhouse, which was built in 1896. Both of these are on Main Street.

Georgina Point Road leads from Miners Bay to Georgina Point (or Active Pass) Lighthouse. On the right, less than 1 kilometre (about 0.5 mile) down the road is the church of St. Mary Magdalene, which was consecrated in 1898. The baptismal font is made of sandstone and weighs 180 kilograms (400 pounds). It was brought over from Saturna Island by rowboat. Where Georgina Point Road meets Waugh Road, turn left and follow the road to the lighthouse, which was constructed in 1885. While the inside of the lighthouse is closed to the public, the grounds are open from 1 PM to 3 PM daily, year-round. It is a great place to go to watch the boats out in Active Pass, to have a picnic or just to take photographs of the lighthouse.

To return to the ferry, you can continue on Waugh Road and go right on Campbell Bay Road and then turn right at Fernhill Road to go back into Miners Bay. From here you can take Village Bay Road the rest of the way to the ferry. Another option is to loop around the southwestern part of the island once you reach Fernhill. There are also a number of other side roads down to bays and coves with docks and beaches.

## GALIANO ISLAND

The ferries arriving on Galiano Island dock at Sturdies Bay. In addition to the ferries from Swartz Bay, there are two per day from Tsawwassen. There is at least one ferry from Long Harbour on Saltspring Island each day of the week, with an extra ferry every weekday except Friday. There are also daily sailings from Mayne, North Pender and Saturna islands. If you are travelling through Active Pass between May and September, watch for pods (extended family groups) of orcas. Usually there are around fifteen whales in a pod but up to sixty-five have been noted in late summer.

The island received its name from Dionisio Alcala Galiano, the Spaniard who sailed through the Strait of Georgia in 1792.

As with most of the Gulf Islands, local Coast Salish Natives had summer camps on Galiano. In fact, Montague Harbour has middens that date back more than three thousand years, proving that the Natives were here many centuries before the non-Natives arrived.

The early European settlers tried farming, growing fruits and vegetables, raising sheep and fishing. There were five different herring-salteries on the island. One of them was operated by Chinese workers and the rest by Japanese immigrants. Japanese owners opened a new saltery and cannery just before the Second World War, but it was taken from them by the government and closed during the Japanese internment.

There are two public campgrounds, one at Montague Harbour Provincial Marine Park and the other at Dionisio Point Provincial Park (walk-in sites only), plus bed-and-breakfasts, inns and lodges throughout the island. The island has no garbage dump, so please take your garbage with you when you leave. A shortage of rainfall during the spring, summer and fall means that campfires are not allowed from April to October.

Galiano is a long and narrow island, reaching 26 kilometres (16 miles) from end to end. From the ferry, you can drive alongside Trincomali Channel right to the other end of the island if you go up Sturdies Bay Road and then turn right onto Porlier Pass Road when you reach it just a few minutes' drive from the ferry. To actually get to Porlier Pass, watch for Cook Road and the signs for Dionisio Point Provincial Park once you near the northern part of the island.

To go to Montague Harbour Provincial Marine Park, turn left off Sturdies Bay Road onto Georgeson Bay Road (instead of right onto Porlier Pass Road) and then right onto Montague Harbour Road. Follow the signs to this park, which has a lovely hiking trail through it. (If you are coming back from North Galiano, turn right onto Clanton and then sharply right again onto the road to the park.)

If you stay on Georgeson Bay Road past Montague Harbour Road, you can turn left onto Bluff Drive to take a gravel road through an old forest along the Galiano Bluffs. Then watch for the road to the right off Bluff Drive to the Bluffs Park summit. From the small parking lot there is a trail leading up along a ridge to the top of Bluff Park. From here you can see Mayne Island to the southeast and Active Pass between the two islands.

Active Pass was named after the *Active*, a two-gun US vessel, the first naval steamer to sail through it, in 1855. While in the park, watch for the large, old cedars— and for the beautiful spring wildflowers if you are here early in the year.

Follow Bluff Drive as it turns left and becomes Burrill Road and then turn right onto the main road at the T junction to return to Sturdies Bay and the ferry.

When you are done touring the Gulf Islands, you can return to Vancouver Island to explore further.

Naniamo

# DUNCAN
# to NANOOSE BAY

*This route takes you northwards along the eastern side of Vancouver Island. You will see lots of the Strait of Georgia and have many opportunities to walk along its shore and swim in its waters. And, although you will cross the 49th Parallel, you will not change countries.*

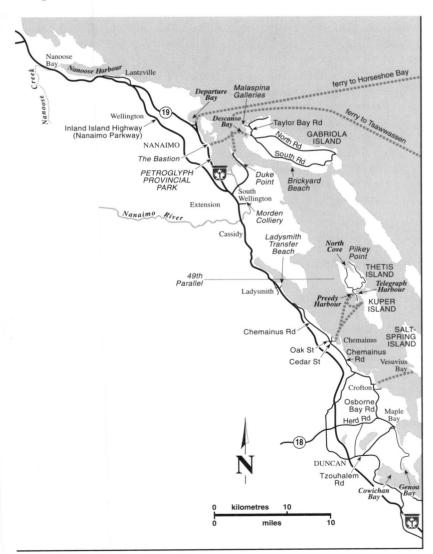

## GENOA BAY & MAPLE BAY

From downtown Duncan (see Chapter 1 for a description of the Duncan area), go eastwards on Trunk Road, which becomes Tzouhalem Road. Continue on Tzouhalem to Maple Bay Road and turn left. You are now on a section of the old Island Highway, the beginning of which is past residences and then beside acreages. The old Island Highway (now Highway 1A) was the first highway up the island. It began as a wagon road from Victoria to Cowichan Bay in 1884.

The old highway bypasses the rush of Highway 1 and takes you past farmland and orchards. It is much more enjoyable to go this way and smell the freshly mowed hay and see the bales in the fields on a summer day. The settlements along this road are mainly resort towns.

As you approach Maple Bay, 5.3 kilometres (3.3 miles) from the beginning of Maple Bay Road, take a side trip by turning right onto Genoa Bay Road. Along this road you pass new homes, marinas and shops before leaving the busy area and driving through farmland. At Genoa Bay you find a small, secluded settlement where many live-aboard boats are moored.

Return to the junction and turn right onto Maple Bay Road. When you reach a stop sign at Herd Road, turn left to go to the town of Crofton. If you want to first visit Maple Bay, which is a more popular bay than Genoa Bay, continue straight ahead. Maple Bay has a roped-off swimming area, store and dock.

## CROFTON

At kilometre 2.7 (mile 1.7) from the beginning of Herd Road, turn right onto Osborne Bay Road. You reach Crofton in about 3.5 kilometres (2.2 miles) from the turn.

As you enter Crofton, you are on York Avenue. Turn right at the first intersection, onto Adelaide, and follow the signs to Osborne Bay Regional Park, a drive of about twenty minutes. At the park you can picnic at the tables, play on the beach or swim in the ocean.

Continue on York Avenue to Joan Street and turn right. At the end of the street on the right there is a 1905 schoolhouse that contains the tourist information booth and the town's museum. The ocean is straight ahead.

Crofton is a small community that overlooks Osborne Bay. It owes its beginning to its deep-sea port, conveniently located to serve the Lenora Mine, which was situated on Mount Sicker to the west of the village. Henry Croft, a director of the newly formed Mount Sicker Copper Mining Company, built a smelter here in 1902 to process the ore from his mine as well as from other producing mines on the mountain. A town, Crofton, was established to house the workers. However, falling copper prices and problems with the smelter caused it to close in 1908 and the town dwindled. Shortly afterwards, the smelter was destroyed by fire.

The railway built to haul the ore to the smelter is said to have been one of the most dangerous and formidable in BC's history. It was such a steep and tightly winding downhill ride that brakemen perched on each of the ore cars so that they could quickly hit the brakes at a moment's notice.

Crofton's deep-sea port is now being used by a pulp and paper mill.

Back on York Avenue, drive one block to a T intersection at Chaplin Street. To the right you will find the government dock and the ferry to Vesuvius Bay on Saltspring Island (see Chapter 4). Go left onto Chaplin Street and in 3.7 kilometres (2.3 miles) you reach a stop sign. Turn right onto Chemainus Road and follow it to the town of Chemainus.

## CHEMAINUS

Chemainus bills itself as 'the Mural Capital of Canada' and 'the Little Town that Did.' Here is the story of Chemainus and its murals:

In the early 1980s, as with most mill towns, lowered lumber production had a devastating effect on the economy of Chemainus. But the residents of the town refused to give up—instead, they painted 12 murals on the walls of local businesses to attract tourists. In 1983, as a result of this determination, the town of Chemainus won the prestigious first-place award in a downtown revitalization competition based in New York. Many communities across the country have copied the idea of painting murals.

**Chief Tzuhalem** *While most of the Natives living on Vancouver Island in the nineteenth century were friendly, Chief Tzuhalem (or Tzouhalem), who was born in the 1790s, was not. However, his anger was directed at his fellow Natives, not the non-Natives. He felt no qualms about murdering anyone who got in his way. He also liked to collect wives—and it did not matter whose.*

*At its largest, Chief Tzuhalem's territory ran from Vancouver Island all the way up the Fraser River to Fort Langley on the mainland and as far south as Tacoma, Washington. He so easily evaded everyone who pursued him that many of his followers thought that he had magical powers. He was finally killed on nearby Kuper Island in 1854 by an irate husband who objected to losing his wife.*

*The story goes that after his death some of the Natives cut open his chest to see if they could discover why he had been such a powerful and wicked man. Inside, it is said, they found a heart that was as small as a salmon's.*

*Today the chief's name lives on not just in the stories of his life, but also in the names of a road in Duncan and a nearby mountain.*

The townspeople kept on painting and the number of murals has now increased to 32. You can see the town's history on display during a stroll through what is called 'the country's largest outdoor art gallery.'

As you come into town on Chemainus Road, find a place to park and tour the outdoor gallery on foot, by pedicab or by horse-drawn wagon.

If you want to walk through 'Old Towne,' continue on Chemainus Road to Spruce Street and turn right. Follow it as it curves right and becomes Alder Street. When

*Chemainus Mural*

*Chemainus Mural*

you cross Willow Street, note Waterwheel Park to your right. Turn left onto Croft Street and park. Then follow the Heritage Path past the museum to Waterwheel Park, where a replica of the waterwheel used in the town's first sawmill is situated. The route continues through the old section of Chemainus and past the seaport. Old Towne was once the business section of Chemainus. The historic buildings are now full of shops of different kinds.

Go back to Chemainus Road and drive further along it until you reach the Pacific Rim Artisan Village, on the corner of Cedar Street. You can recognize it by the huge pink archway on the left. Here you can admire contemporary fine art, various exhibitions and crafts and perhaps find something to buy.

In the flower-bed at the left end of the arch there is a sculpture of 'the Hermit' pushing a wheelbarrow. No one knows where Charlie Abbott, 'the Hermit,' came from. He spent years clearing the paths, building walls and planting flowers on the piece of land that is now known as 'the Hermit Trails.' School children on field trips here years ago would spend as much time looking about hoping to catch sight of him as they would looking at his work. Though he was a very private person and few people ever saw him, he created these trails and flower-beds on the outskirts of Chemainus as much for others to enjoy (as long as they left him alone) as for his own pleasure. After Charlie died in 1989, his trails were taken over as a public park.

To get to the trails, drive about 100 metres (300 feet) along Cedar Street past the archway until you come to some baseball diamonds on your right. Turn right into the parking area and continue to drive between the chain-link fences of the diamonds. Look ahead and to the right for a narrow road into the trees. Park beside the fence and then walk briefly along the narrow road until you reach a road to the left. Go down it to the Y, take the right fork, and enter the Hermit Trails.

From the entrance there are three trails to choose from. They are all pleasant to walk on and each one has something unique. You could easily spend half a day wandering around here.

Back at Chemainus Road, turn left. Drive past Fir Street and turn right onto Oak Street at the sign for the Thetis Island Ferry.

## THETIS ISLAND

The ferry from Chemainus to Thetis Island leaves every two hours. Some of the ferries go directly to Thetis and some stop in at the Indian reserve on adjacent Kuper Island.

Thetis is small—only 6 kilometres (4 miles) long and 3 kilometres (2 miles) wide. The island has only one resort, one bed-and-breakfast and no public campground. Most of the services are at Telegraph Harbour. During the summer months there is usually a shortage of water on the island, so please use it wisely.

*Charlie Abbott tending the trail*

Three of the early families to settle on Thetis Island were the Hunters, who arrived in 1891 and made North Cove their home; the Burcells, who moved to Preedy Harbour in 1892; and the Heneages, who arrived in 1904. The Hunters and Burcells owned most of the island. The Burcells opened a store and built a large home near today's ferry dock, naming it 'Preedy Hall.'

The original Preedy Hall was sold by Mrs. Burcell and burned down soon after. It was rebuilt in 1930 and is now part of the Capernwray Harbour Bible Camp, one of the three Christian study groups that now own a large portion of the island.

Camp Columbia, a children's summer camp, was opened by the Anglican Church in 1947. It was set up on land left to the church by Major Alfred Heneage upon his death. The major and his sister, Eveline Mary, put in a vegetable garden and an English flower garden while they lived here.

The last of the three camps, Pioneer Pacific Children's Camp, is run by the Intervarsity Christian Fellowship, on land donated by the Hunter family.

All land on the island is private. For public access to the beach, go to the end of Pilkey Point Road.

## SALTAIR & LADYSMITH

Back on the old Island Highway, Chemainus Road, you travel through Saltair, a community that stretches out along the road, on the way to Ladysmith. You drive beside the Strait of Georgia as the road winds it way past orchards, acreages, crops of corn and pasture.

At kilometre 8.2 (mile 5) from the Thetis Island ferry you reach Highway 1. Turn right and then right again in 1.3 kilometres (0.8 miles) to take Oyster Cove Road. Go down it to Ladysmith Transfer Beach Park, a nice big public park on the Stuart Channel. Here you can swim in what is claimed to be some of the warmest salt water north of San Francisco or have a picnic while the children play in the playground. (The name of the beach may have come about because coal was once transferred to ships here.)

Just after you get back onto the highway you are in Ladysmith. This town was built in 1898 to provide deep-water loading of coal sent by rail from the town of Extension, 17.7 kilometres (11 miles) to the northwest. It was also used as a place for the miners to get away from the dust of the mines. The first houses were vacant ones brought in

*49ᵗʰ Parallel at Ladysmith*

from Wellington, located between where Nanaimo and Lantzville now are, 32 kilometres (20 miles) to the northwest. They were sawn into sections and loaded onto rail-cars. Once at Ladysmith, they were nailed back together. Some are still being used today. After the need for coal declined, logging became a major industry and so the harbour is now being used for loading logs onto ships.

Drive along the highway to Gatacre Street and turn left. In one block, you reach 1st Avenue. On the right corner, a tall, yellow building that used to be the Jones Hotel is now the Black Nugget Museum.

Go along 1st Avenue in either direction to see the restored historic buildings of the business section of the town. You can see them better if you park and go on foot. If you like antiques, there are a number of shops to visit.

The houses adjoining the business area are in quaint, early twentieth-century styles. They get progressively newer the farther you go.

As you drive out of town, watch for the huge 'Ladysmith' sign on the 49th Parallel. The 49th Parallel, the invisible line that marks most of the boundary between western Canada and the United States, runs through Ladysmith. However, as a result of negotiations, Vancouver Island remained wholly in Canada.

The boundary between western Canada and the United States was set at the 49th Parallel of Latitude by the Oregon Treaty in 1846. This boundary line can easily be drawn on a map but there is no physical feature, such as a river or ridgeline, to mark it—it is considered to be 'topographically absurd.' Of Canada's ten provincial capitals, only three are north of the 49th Parallel. Even Ottawa, the country's capital, is south of the dividing line.

## CASSIDY

Cassidy was established in 1917 as a coal town. It was named after Tom Cassidy, a farmer from Iowa who settled here in 1878. Modern for its time, it had streetlights, running water and sewers. By 1928, an average of about 900 tonnes (1000 tons) of coal was being taken out of the mine during each eight-hour shift. However, in 1932 the mine shut down on account of four factors: the growing use of oil, the seam of coal running out, the mine becoming too dangerous and the Depression.

One of the sad stories of the closing recounts how an old Chinese worker, fearing that he would not get a job anywhere else, hanged himself in the shaft house.

For a close-up look at relics of the coal mining in the area, turn right onto Morden Road, 12.1 kilometres (7.5 miles) north of Cassidy. At the four-way stop, go straight ahead. The road curves to the left and becomes gravel. When you reach the Y, go right and at kilometre 0.9 (mile 0.6) from the highway, you reach the last remaining 'tipple' on Vancouver Island. (A tipple is a structure built over a mine shaft to hold the machinery that raises the coal cars to the surface and then empties them by tipping.)

The tipple here at the Morden Colliery is 23 metres (75 feet) high and has stood up so well over time because it is made of concrete and steel and is thus completely fireproof. It was the first of its type in the area.

Coal mining began at the Morden mine in 1912. It had a production of about 1360 tonnes (1500 tons) per nine-hour shift. After years of strikes and shutdowns on account of explosive gas leaks and flooding, the mine closed in 1921. It reopened in 1930 for a short time before closing once again.

*Morden mine*

Just north of Morden Road, the highway runs through South Wellington, which was also a coal town.

## NANAIMO

As you approach Nanaimo, stop in at Petroglyph Provincial Park, at the south end of the city. It is located right beside the highway into downtown, about 2 kilometres (1.3 miles) past the overpass for the Nanaimo Parkway. A petroglyph is a picture, usually prehistoric, which has been hammered or chipped in a rock. The carvings are on a sandstone ridge overlooking the harbour.

These carvings in the park were done hundreds of years ago by the Natives of the area. There are human figures, birds, fish and animals. Their meanings, however, are no longer known.

*Note:* To protect the originals from further vandalism and natural wearing away—and to give you a better idea of what they looked like without this damage—the petroglyphs that you are looking at are actually casts of the originals.

In 1791 the Spanish arrived at what is now Nanaimo and found the Native community of Sney-Ny-mos, which in the Native tongue meant 'where the big tribe dwells' or 'a big, strong tribe.' It got its name because it was the centre for five Native bands.

Later, the English came to the area and began to explore for resources that they could profit from. In 1852, some Natives brought the Hudson's Bay Company workers a few black lumps. The company men recognized the material and by the end of that year they had shipped out 480 barrels of coal.

### Robert & James Dunsmuir

*Robert Dunsmuir arrived on Vancouver Island from Scotland in 1851 with his wife Joan, two daughters and one son, James. At first Robert worked as the Hudson's Bay Company foreman at its coal mine at Fort Rupert, at the northern end of Vancouver Island (see Chapter 9). The mine soon failed and he was transferred to the Nanaimo workings. When not on the job for the Hudson's Bay Company, he was searching for coal on his own.*

*One day in the early 1870s he found an outcropping of coal, which was the beginning of his empire. James Dunsmuir began managing and increasing his father's business in 1876. The two contracted to build the Esquimalt and Nanaimo Railway in 1883 and received $750,000 and almost one-quarter of Vancouver Island as payment.*

*Both men were known for hiring cheap labour and for their dislike of unions. Each man also spent time in political office: Robert was elected MLA for Nanaimo in 1882 and again in 1886; James was premier of BC from 1900 to 1902 and later became lieutenant-governor.*

*Robert died in 1889, while his mansion, Craigdarroch Castle, was still under construction in Victoria. James in turn built Hatley Castle, a sister to Craigdarroch, overlooking Esquimalt Harbour (see Chapter 3). He died in 1920.*

The Hudson's Bay Company men must have feared for their safety, because in 1853 they built a bastion (a kind of fortification) near the waterfront to protect themselves from Native attacks. However, not one shot was fired from it, other than for ceremonial purposes. This bastion is the oldest Hudson's Bay Company fort in North America that survives as an original rather than as a reconstruction. Every day at noon you can watch 'the Bastion guards' in their nineteenth-century clothing fire the fort's gun.

Nanaimo was incorporated as a city in 1874 and is the third oldest city in British Columbia.

The city has the distinction of being 'the Bathtub Capital of Canada.' It has an average of three and one-half bathtubs per home. Maybe because of this abundance of tubs, the city hosts an annual bathtub race the last Sunday in July.

It begins at Swy-a-lana Lagoon, behind the civic arena on the Nanaimo Harbour. Participants race for about one and one-half hours in motorized bathtubs through the Strait of Georgia, to the finish line at nearby Departure Bay. While the race used to be across the strait to Vancouver, its new course is less dangerous and makes it easier for people to see both the start and finish of the race.

If you are in Nanaimo between November and April, go down to the ocean and see the Steller's and California sea lions that have come to feed on the spawning herring.

As you drive through Nanaimo, watch for the signs for the ferry to Gabriola Island. It leaves from its own dock right downtown on Nanaimo Harbour (whereas the ferry to Horseshoe Bay leaves from Departure Bay to the north of downtown and the ferry to Tsawwassen leaves from the terminal at Duke Point, to the east across the Nanaimo River Estuary).

## GABRIOLA ISLAND

*Malaspina Galleries, Gabriola*

The ferry to Gabriola Island, which runs every hour from 6 AM to 11 PM, arrives at Descanso Bay.

The island is about 14 kilometres (9 miles) long. While there are two private campgrounds, there is no camping at any of the three provincial parks. Along both the north and south shores there are a number of beach accesses.

The Coast Salish Natives used to visit the southern end of the island in summer to hunt and fish. Of the non-Native settlers who began to arrive, many who turned to farming on this island had previously worked in the coal mines of Nanaimo. Others found work in the sandstone quarry south of Descanso Bay. The quarry, which opened in 1887, shipped building blocks to Victoria. In 1932 it began producing huge grindstones that were bought by paper mills and used to crush wood chips into pulp.

Gabriola is famous for a particular natural sandstone formation, the Malaspina Galleries. To visit them, turn left onto Taylor Bay Road just after you start up the hill from the ferry. Follow this road until you

*Malaspina Galleries*

see signs for the galleries, then turn left onto Malaspina Drive, a country lane with lots of trees and few houses.

Park in the lot at the end of the road. Look for the sign indicating public access and follow the narrow path beside a fence down to the shore. The galleries were formed over the centuries by wind and wave erosion and were a sacred and spiritual place for Native people in the area. The galleries are about 4 metres (13 feet) high and stretch for about 100 metres (330 feet) along the shore. Walk their length and enjoy their intriguing and unworldly appearance.

The galleries were made famous by Dionisio Alcala Galiano, who drew sketches of the formations and took them back to Europe. The drawings reminded the Spaniards of the cloisters or walking galleries of Europe, which typically had a wall on one side and were open on the other, hence the name 'gallery' for the sandstone formation.

The formation was for a time known as 'the Galiano Gallery,' in honour of the man who sketched them. However, he was at the time in the employ of a well-known Italian explorer, Malaspina, and it was the latter's name that was eventually commemorated here. While in the service of Spain, Malaspina lent two of his officers, Galiano and Valdes, and his schooners the *Sutil* and the *Mexicana*, to that country. The two men replaced an injured Spanish explorer on the voyage to explore the northwest coast of the New World and so went on to become renowned for their explorations of the British Columbia coast in 1792.

Brickyard Beach, located around the middle of the southern side of the island, got its name from a brickyard that operated here between 1895 and 1945. Its workers were mainly Chinese and the bricks were hauled to Descanso Bay to be shipped to Vancouver Island.

The shortest route to this beach is to go back towards to the ferry and to continue up the hill on North Road from Taylor Bay Road and then go right at the fork to take South Road until you get there. North and South roads connect again at

*Malaspina Galleries*

the other end of the island, so you can take a pleasant drive all the way around the island if you like.

As you line up on Taylor Bay Road to take a departing ferry, look for the sign that marks the dividing line between cars that can expect to get onto the next ferry and those that will have to wait for the following one. If you are sitting in your hot vehicle in a long line-up, look towards the little green lagoon just across from the White Hart Pub. It is just a few steps to some rocks overlooking the lagoon—a cool, very serene and beautiful place to wait for the ferry.

## LANTZVILLE & NANOOSE BAY

At Nanaimo, Highway 1 crosses the Strait of Georgia (via ferry) to North Vancouver. As you leave Nanaimo heading northwards you are now on Highway 19.

If you want to take a nice, picturesque drive through the ocean-side hamlet of Lantzville, turn right onto Lantzville Road (at the intersection with the Nanaimo Parkway) once you leave the city limits of Nanaimo. It is downhill into the town and the main street is lined with trees. From this road you can admire the older homes with their beautiful, colourful yards and you can see the ships out in Nanoose Harbour.

In 5 kilometres (3 miles) you are back at Highway 19 and a short distance along the highway you near the settlement of Nanoose Bay.

The Nanoose Natives were already living here long before the Spaniards arrived in 1791. Then, during the 1850s, the fur traders came through. In 1863, John Enos became the first settler in the area by building his home on Notch Hill. When you see the rest area on the left, look to your right to see Nanoose Bay, which is part of Nanoose Harbour, and across it, Notch Hill.

Later, the hill was the site of a giant powder works, and was used as a Canadian Navy test range. A settlement on the side of the harbour where the highway now runs was called 'Red Gap.'

Then you cross Nanoose Creek and 2.7 kilometres (1.6 miles) farther up the highway you pass the Family Fun Park on the left. Your children will want to ride in the go-carts, see the huge fly or try one of the games in the large yard.

From here, you can continue northwards up the Island Highway and either head for the west coast of the island via Highway 4 at Parksville (see Chapter 6), or keep right on going up the east coast (see Chapters 6-9).

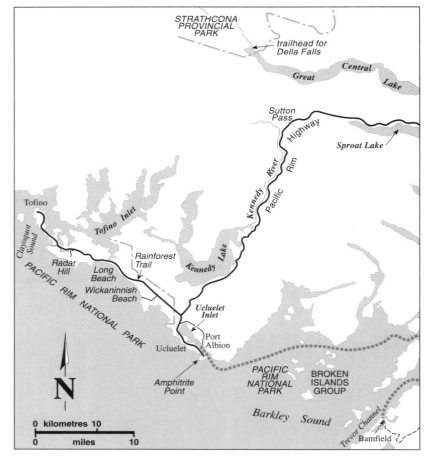

STRATHCONA
PROVINCIAL
PARK

trailhead for
Della Falls

Great    Central
Lake

Sutton
Pass

Highway

Sproat Lake

Kennedy River

Pacific Rim

Tofino

Tofino Inlet

Clayoquot Sound

Rainforest
Trail

Kennedy Lake

Radar
Hill

Long
Beach

PACIFIC RIM NATIONAL PARK

Wickaninnish
Beach

Ucluelet
Inlet

Port
Albion

Ucluelet

Amphitrite
Point

PACIFIC
RIM
NATIONAL
PARK

BROKEN
ISLANDS
GROUP

Barkley    Sound

Trevor Channel

Bamfield

0    kilometres  10

0         miles        10

N

# PARKSVILLE
# to TOFINO

*This route is full of contrasts. At Parksville, on the east coast of Vancouver Island, you can walk along the loose, sandy beach of the Strait of Georgia. From Parksville you will cut across to the west coast of the island. On the way you will see goats on a rooftop, a tea house in a tree and a bog close to a rainforest. When you arrive on the west coast, you can stroll on the hard-packed sand of Long Beach and swim in the Pacific Ocean.*

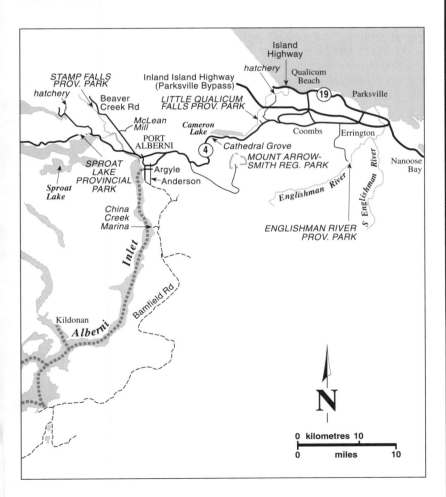

## PARKSVILLE

Drive northwards from Nanaimo along Highway 19 and as you come into Parksville, you can see a seawall on the right. Stop at one of the parking areas if you would like to enjoy a stroll along it. The beach at Parksville is claimed to have 'the warmest water in all of

*Paradise Adventures Park*

Canada' as a result of the sun warming the sand when the tide is out and the hot sand heating the water when the tide returns.

Parksville was first known as 'The River,' because of the nearby Englishman River. When the road from the south reached the small settlement, a post office was opened. The postmaster was Mr. Nelson Parks and the town was eventually named after him.

Every April, over twenty thousand brant geese return to the area and the residents hold a three-day Brant Festival to celebrate the occasion. Brant geese are small sea geese that do a lot of chattering. There are viewing stations along the beach to watch the geese as they arrive.

Every year, on the last weekend of July, Parksville also holds its International Sandcastle Competition. Participants have only the time from when the tide goes out until it comes in again to sculpt their creations.

Paradise Adventures Mini Golf and RV Park is at the northern end of the city. The yard has a castle, a waterwheel, a large shoe, an old ship and an abundance of flowers. It is a lovely place to spend time with your children.

To continue on towards Port Alberni and Tofino, turn onto Highway 4 where it meets Highway 19 in downtown Parksville and stay on it as you cross over the Inland Island Highway.

*Note:* If, as you come up the Island Highway, you want to bypass Parksville and head straight for the west coast, take the turn-off for the Parksville Bypass/Inland Island Highway before you reach Parksville. Craig Heritage Park, on the right,

*Paradise Adventures Park*

1.6 kilometres (1 mile) from the junction, has a small log building that was constructed in 1888 and used as a post office until 1912, a 1946 fire-engine in a 1942 fire-hall, a church built in 1912 and lots of old machinery. Then take the exit for Highway 4 westbound at the interchange.

## ERRINGTON & COOMBS

As you drive along Highway 4, the Alberni Highway, watch for the sign for Englishman River Falls Provincial Park and turn left onto Errington Road. In 1.9 kilometres (1.1 miles) from the highway you reach a four-way stop in the village of Errington. If you are here on a Saturday between 10 AM and 1 PM, stop in at the farmers' market.

Continue straight ahead to reach the entrance to the park 6.2 kilometres (3.9 miles) from the stop sign in Errington. Go past the campground to the Upper Falls parking lot.

Look at the map here to see how to get to the falls. It also warns you about the dangerous cliffs, but the path is wide and easy to walk. You can hear the roar of the water as you approach the falls.

In a 1 kilometre (0.5 mile) stretch of the Englishman River, there are two waterfalls, a deep canyon and clear pools of water. If you would like to take a brisk swim, try the lower pool.

**Living off the Land** *The First Nations of Vancouver Island have traditionally consisted of three different groups: in the southeast, the Coast Salish; on the west coast, the Nuu-chah-nulth (Nootka); and in the north, the Kwakwa'ka'wakw (Kwakiutl or Kwagiulth).*

*When the non-Natives first came to Vancouver Island, the different Native groups had already long since developed their own ways of living off the land.*

*The Coast Salish constructed weirs to catch their fish and dug for clams. They also ate birds, which they caught by stringing nets on poles high in the air. Many plants provided them with medicines. Devil's club, for instance, was used to relieve rheumatism and arthritis.*

*For much of their food, the Nuu-chah-nulth headed out onto the ocean, where they hunted the migrating humpback and gray whales from canoes. They used floats as drags to tire a whale that they had harpooned. When it rose to the surface, they killed it. The harpoon blades were made from elk antlers or mussel shells.*

*The Nuu-chah-nulth also gathered food on land. For example, individual families would own certain patches of wild salmonberry, from which they would pick what they needed before letting other members of the band help themselves to what was left. They also dried thimbleberries with smoked clams to keep through the winter.*

*The Kwakwa'ka'wakw dried their meat over fires fueled by redcedar, because of that wood's almost smoke-free burn. They started their fires with friction, using a redcedar drill and hearth. Because of these and many other uses, the redcedar was 'the tree of life' to the Kwakwa'ka'wakw.*

*The Kwakwa'ka'wakw were foremost among the artists of the First Nations of the region. Before they could become sculptors, weavers or painters, the young people had to apprentice for many years. Their works include masks, totems and raven rattles.*

Go back to Highway 4 and turn left. In 3.5 kilometres (2.2 miles) you reach the village of Coombs, which began as a stopover on the stagecoach trail to Alberni.

*Englishman River falls*

The Coombs General Store is on the left of the highway. It has 'Coachlines Agent,' 'Provisions,' 'Post Office' and 'Hardware' printed on its front. Park on the right of the highway and walk through the rest of the hamlet.

Just across the street from the general store there is an old log house where they sell antiques and down the highway from the log house is Frontier Town, a must stop. It is full of little shops, some with modern items and all with an old frontier-town atmosphere. You can have coffee and ice cream, visit a 'rubber stamp farm' and see antler carvings, collectibles and antiques.

Past Frontier Town is the Old Country Market, a long building with a sod roof. Check on the roof for the goats that keep it trimmed—usually a mama and two or three little ones. They make a lot of noise as they trot around bleating. Inside you can buy flowers, vegetables and fruits, depending on the season.

As you leave Coombs, you cross a bridge and then to the left there is a smokery where you can buy smoked salmon. Once you pass the rodeo grounds, you can visit Butterfly World if you turn left onto Winchester Road and then immediately go right onto the Old Alberni Highway.

Inside Butterfly World there is a tropical garden with multi-coloured butterflies fluttering about. There are also Chinese quail on the ground and songbirds in the trees. You can wander along the wooden walkways inside enjoying the pools with turtles and fish, waterfalls and lush vegetation or stroll outside to see the water gardens.

*Coombs*

Back on the highway and after 0.5 kilometre (0.3 mile) you come to a junction with Highway 4A. To the right is Qualicum Beach. Turn left to go to Port Alberni. There are shops and cafes along this road for the next 7 kilometres (4 miles).

*Goats on roof, Old Country Market*

## LITTLE QUALICUM RIVER FALLS & MACMILLAN PARK

In 4 kilometres (2.5 miles) from the junction, you reach Melrose Road, which leads to the Little Qualicum River Fish Hatchery—a drive of 7.5 kilometres (4.7 miles). Before turning, however, read the sign that states whether there are any fish to see.

Then, at kilometre 6.7 (mile 4.2), you get to Little Qualicum Falls Road, which leads to Little Qualicum Falls Provincial Park. From the parking lot, head to the picnic area. The trail to the Lower Falls is at the end of the picnic area. It is downhill, on steps and pathways, all the way. You come to a point where there is set of wooden steps to the left. Here there is a map of the trails in the park and the paths to the falls. Go right to reach the Lower Falls, or left up the steps to get to the Upper Falls.

On the way to the Lower Falls you come to a bridge across the canyon. You can see where the swirl of the river over the years has smoothed out the rock and made potholes or pools in it. The waterfall itself is small, with cascades before and after it.

*Little Qualicum River Falls*

To reach the Upper Falls, you walk along a path high above the river (fenced for safety). Down below you can see small cascades. The Upper Falls is higher than the Lower Falls and also has 'potholes.'

Back on Highway 4, in 4 kilometres (2.5 miles) you reach the Cameron Lake picnic grounds, where you can stop and enjoy your lunch along the lake. Try fishing for trout while you are here. As you resume your drive towards Port Alberni, you continue to see Cameron Lake to your right. It is a lovely view with the mountains across the water.

When you notice that you have been driving between tall Douglas-fir trees, that is an indication that you are nearing MacMillan Park's

Cathedral Grove

Cathedral Grove. Park in the lot on either side of the road and walk amongst the trees—the best trail is on the southeastern (left) side of the highway.

*Note:* Trees or their branches can die from root and stem diseases. Branches or whole trees sometimes fall without warning, and so you are advised not to walk these paths on windy days.

Some of the Douglas-firs in the park are eight hundred years old but most of the trees here sprouted after a fire ravaged the forest about three hundred years ago. With much of the easily accessible old-growth forest on Vancouver Island having been logged, this remaining stand of old-growth forest is priceless, so no smoking is allowed in the park.

It is an easy walk to get to the Cathedral Grove that gives the park its name, a first-growth stand of Douglas-fir that survived the fire. As you stroll along the dim and cool trails, you have to look way up to see the tops of these very tall, old trees.

There are signs along the way that offer explanations about the trees that you see. A sign in front of a tree with the base of its trunk about half a metre (1.5 feet) off the ground reads:

### Trees on Stilts
*This western hemlock began life along with hundreds of others as seedlings on a fallen log. Although most of its neighbours perished, it was able*

*to survive at a slow growth for many years. Gradually it sent its roots groping to the forest floor. As the log decayed, these roots were left exposed. Today this sturdy tree remains looking as if it were standing on stilts.*

Another sign, at a Douglas-fir:

### The Douglas-fir

*The dominant tree of this trail, the Douglas-fir, is Canada's largest growing tree. Long lived, tough, and durable, it is known for its phenomenal growth rate. A fire destroyed all but a few giant trees in this forest more than 300 years ago. Protected from the heat by thick, corky bark, the surviving veterans provided the seeds that have grown into the present forest.*

The Douglas-fir was named after David Douglas, a botanist who explored Oregon, Washington and BC in the 1800s. It is considered to be the third-tallest species of tree in North America; only the redwood and Sitka spruce have been found to grow taller. The largest Douglas-fir in the park is 3 metres (9.8 feet) in diameter.

The area was donated to the people of the province in 1944 by Harvey Reginald MacMillan. He was a philanthropist, forester and sportsman. MacMillan was, from the time of its founding in 1919, the head of the forestry company that, upon his retirement from the role, merged with Bloedel, Stewart and Welch in 1951, to form the giant timber, pulp and paper company MacMillan Bloedel.

After you leave the parking lot, you continue driving past tall trees for the next 3.8 kilometres (2.4 miles). After the tall trees, you begin to climb and at kilometre 7.4 (mile 4.6) from the parking lot, you reach the Alberni Summit at an elevation of 375 metres (1230 feet). You are on Mount Arrowsmith, which is part of the Beaufort Range.

## MOUNT ARROWSMITH & PORT ALBERNI

You then start descending steeply and in 1.4 kilometres (0.8 mile) from the summit you reach the turn-off for Mount Arrowsmith Regional Park. The park has lovely alpine meadows to see in the summer and a downhill ski facility that operates in the winter. Since the trails and roads are not always maintained, check with the tourist information booth in Port Alberni before venturing in if you are in doubt.

It is a long, curving descent to Port Alberni at the eastern end of the Alberni Inlet.

'Welcome to the Alberni Valley, Salmon Capital of the World, Gateway to the Pacific Rim,' reads the sign at a Y where the highway splits into two local roads. Johnston Road bears to the right. Take the Port Alberni Highway to the left and then turn right into the tourist information booth parking lot. You can find weather forecasts and

*Clocktower, Port Alberni*

## Alberni Inlet

*Alberni Inlet is 40 kilometres (25 miles) long and reaches a depth of 343 metres (1125 feet). One of the longest inlets on Vancouver Island, it starts at Barkley Sound, between Bamfield and Ucluelet, and almost cuts the island in half as it runs to the northeast. It was carved by glaciers and then filled with ocean water when they melted.*

*For thousands of years, local Natives used the inlet as a haven from cold weather in the winter, as a camp for catching the salmon that returned up the inlet to their spawning rivers and to get away from the sometimes-rough ocean. The European arrivals looked upon it in the same way and also saw a bright future for logging. One day in 1964, however, the calm of the inlet was shattered as a tidal wave blasted up the narrow inlet. Caused by an earthquake in Anchorage, Alaska, it sent water, logs, boats and debris onto the streets of Port Alberni, destroying houses and other buildings.*

whale-watching reports for Long Beach here, as well as a detailed trail map for Pacific Rim National Park, which this route also visits.

The name 'Alberni' comes from Don Pedro Alberni, who led a Spanish exploring party to the area in 1790 and who was in command of the fort at Nootka when the Spanish occupied it in 1791.

Port Alberni is set amidst great tracts of forest and offers a sheltered deep-sea port at the northern end of Alberni Inlet. It was, therefore, an appropriate place to build, in 1861, the first sawmill in British Columbia set up especially for cutting export lumber. Then, in 1947, one of Canada's most productive pulp and paper mills was opened here.

Continue on past the tourist information booth towards downtown as the road becomes Redford Street. Go to 3rd Avenue, at a set of traffic lights, and turn left. Drive about half a dozen blocks to Argyle and turn right. At the end of the road you arrive at the Alberni Harbour Quay.

At the quay there is a brick-paved square lined with many shops and restaurants. Stop in at the market square or the Forestry Visitors Centre. If you would like to overlook the marina and the waters of the inlet, go to the clock tower and climb its five short flights of stairs to the viewpoint.

The *MV Lady Rose* and the *MV Frances Barkley* leave this quay for (respectively) Bamfield or Ucluelet. The *Lady Rose* carries one hundred passengers, in addition to its freight and mail, while the *Frances Barkley* can carry two hundred passengers. Take along a sweater or jacket as it might be cold on the water. These trips are popular, so book ahead (phone 1-800-663-7192) and be at the quay early—they leave at 8 AM. At publication time, a round trip to Bamfield on the *MV Lady Rose* returns at 5:30 PM and costs $40 per person, while a similar excursion to Ucluelet on the *MV Frances Barkley* returns by 7 PM and costs $44.

The *Lady Rose* goes to Bamfield on Tuesdays, Thursdays and Saturdays, stopping in at the settlement of Kildonan on the way. If you go to Bamfield on a day-trip, you will have one hour to one and one-half hours to tour the village before returning. During the summer, there are also trips on Fridays and Sundays.

From June 1 and throughout the summer on Mondays, Wednesdays and Fridays, the *Frances Barkley* cruises to the Sechart Whaling Station, through the Broken

Island Group, to Ucluelet, where you have a one-hour stopover. Whales are no longer hunted here and the whaling station is now the site of a lodge (reserve when you book a cruise) and is a drop-off point for kayakers headed for the Broken Group. The Broken Islands Group contains over one hundred islands and islets. As you sail through Barkley Sound, watch for orcas, gray whales, seals, river otters and porpoises in the water and for bald eagles in the sky.

If you would like to go windsurfing on Alberni Inlet, drive back up Argyle to Anderson (13th) Avenue and turn right. Stay on it as it becomes Bamfield Road and about 14 kilometres (9 miles) down this gravel road from Argyle there is a turn-off on the right for the China Creek Marina. Here you can rent windsurfing equipment. Because the water up the inlet warms in the sun and the water closer to the ocean remains cold, there are thermal winds here that make windsurfing in the early afternoon especially exciting. (If you continue along Bamfield Road, you will reach Franklin Headquarters and Camp and hook up with roads to Bamfield and Cowichan Lake—see Chapter 2.)

When you are ready to leave town, take 3rd Avenue northwards from Argyle Street and continue past Redford and Roger streets to Johnston Road (Highway 4) and turn left. Get into the right-hand lane, drive two blocks, turn right at the next set of lights and immediately cross a bridge over a tributary of the Somass River. Just after the bridge you come to a Y where Highway 4 continues to the left and Beaver Creek Road branches off to the right and runs part of the way up the Alberni Basin, which is up to 11 kilometres (7 miles) wide and 40 kilometres (25 miles) long.

To see a restored 1920s steam-operated sawmill and the rest of the sights at McLean Mill National Historic Site, drive up Beaver Creek Road for 5.9 kilometres (3.7 miles) to Smith Road and turn right. In a further 3.1 kilometres (1.9 miles), you reach the historic site.

The McLean Mill is the last steam-operated sawmill in the province. It ceased operation in 1965, after forty years of sawing logs. The McLeans donated the mill, buildings and machinery to Port Alberni in 1985 and it was declared a national historic site in 1989 by the Historical Sites and Monuments Board of Canada. Five years later, MacMillan Bloedel donated an additional 12 hectares (30 acres) of land around the 1-hectare (2.4-acre) original site.

A major restoration has taken place over the years and much of the machinery is operating. Besides the steam-powered sawmill, you can see 35 buildings, including the McLean residence. Also of interest are a fish ladder and a pond, a steam donkey and other heavy equipment and a short railway siding. The site is open Monday to Friday, from 8:30 AM to 3:30 PM.

If you continue up Beaver Creek Road for 7.2 kilometres (4.5 miles), you can visit Stamp Falls Provincial Park and hike to the falls, swim in the river or picnic under the trees. September is the best time if you wish to see the salmon make their way upstream to spawn, bypassing the falls with the help of a fish ladder.

*Petroglyphs, Sproat Lake*

## GREAT CENTRAL LAKE, DELLA FALLS & SPROAT LAKE

Return to the Y where Beaver Creek Road diverges from Highway 4 and turn right onto Highway 4 and drive along it, with the Somass River on your left. When you reach another Y, at Falls Road, keep left to cross the Somass River. After the bridge, watch for the Treehouse Teahouse on your right. It is a 74-square-metre (800-square-foot) building up in a tree. Stop in there so that you can say that you had tea in a treehouse. It is open from 9:30 AM to 6 PM.

The section of Highway 4 that you are now on, the Pacific Rim Highway, was paved in 1972. You soon cross the Sproat River and in 1.9 kilometres (1.1 miles) from the crossing you reach the turn-off for Great Central Lake Road to the right.

Turn onto this road to visit a fish hatchery, to go to Great Central Lake and, if you are a hardy outdoors-person, to hike to Della Falls. The short side road to Robertson Creek Fish Hatchery is to the right at 6.8 kilometres (4.2 miles) from the highway. At the hatchery, which is on the Stamp River, hundreds of thousands of steelhead trout and coho and chinook salmon are released into the Stamp-Somass river system each year. The hatchery is open to the public year-round from 8 AM to 4 PM.

You arrive at 35-kilometre (22-mile) long Great Central Lake 1 kilometre (0.6 mile) past the turn-off for the hatchery. You can swim or water-ski here, or try fishing for Kamloops and cutthroat trout. You can rent a boat at Ark Resort on the lakeshore.

To get to the trailhead for Della Falls at the other end of the lake, you can take your own or a rented boat or a water taxi. With a total height of 440 metres

(1443 feet) for its three cascades, Della Falls, located in Strathcona Provincial Park, is the second-highest waterfall in Canada. It was discovered by Joe Drinkwater and named by him for his wife.

It takes a total of 2–4 days to do the 16-kilometre (10-mile) hike if you traverse the lake by motor boat; if you are canoeing or kayaking, set aside 4–7 days. Watch out for bears as you hike, and take note that this trail should not be undertaken by beginner hikers. The trail starts by following Drinkwater Creek on an old road bed and crosses many side creeks on logs or well-maintained bridges. The first 11 kilometres (7 miles) are basically flat, but the trail begins to climb after crossing the Drinkwater Creek Gorge. Near the end there are side trails that lead to Love Lake and Della Lake. (You can read more about the rest of Strathcona Provincial Park in Chapter 8.)

Just up Highway 4 from the road to Great Central Lake, there is a turn-off to the left for Sproat Lake Provincial Park. Go to the parking lot at the picnic area on the lake. From the picnic area, walk down to the beach and look out onto the lake.

Originally built for the Second World War, the Martin Mars planes parked here have been converted into the world's largest water bombers. They can carry up to 27,300 litres (6000 imperial gallons or 7200 US gallons) of water for fighting fires. Their wingspan is 61 metres (200 feet), their tailwings are almost five storeys high and their overall length is 36.6 metres (120 feet). Ask at the tanker base if you are interested in a tour.

While you are at the beach area, look for the sign pointing to your left, where there are some petroglyphs. Follow the 500-metre (550-yard) sand-and-gravel path along the lakeshore to its end and go out onto the small dock. Then look at the lower part of the adjacent rock wall to see the petroglyphs. They are getting faint but you can still make them out.

Continue along the Pacific Rim Highway as it follows Sproat Lake and at kilometre 17.5 (mile 10.9) from the park there is a stop-of-interest sign to the left. The write-up is about Gilbert Malcolm Sproat, after whom the lake is named. Following his arrival in the area in 1860, he helped build the first sawmill in Port Alberni and then held various government offices until 1889, when he retired.

Also here is a hiking trail with a forestry company sign encouraging you to hike through the trees to see what is happening in the forest. On this short hike you can see various species of

*Water bombers, Sproat Lake*

Rocks near Long Beach

trees at different stages of growth—some are identified and others are not—and the stumps of trees that were logged. It is an enjoyable walk even if you have no interest in botany or forestry practices.

The road begins climbing and you reach Sutton Pass, with an elevation of 175 metres (574 feet), at kilometre 37 (mile 23) from the park. Sutton Pass is on the dividing line between rivers that flow to the east and those that flow to the west on this part of Vancouver Island. After the pass, you begin descending into the Kennedy River Canyon. There are canyon walls to the left and the Kennedy River and the opposite canyon walls to the right. Stop at the pull-out 9.2 kilometres (5.7 miles) from the summit if you want to climb the huge, square boulders in the river or lie on them in the sunshine.

All along this section of highway there are signs that tell you when each cut-block was logged, when it was replanted and when it will be cut again. At kilometre 45.2 (mile 28.1) there is 'a Walk in the Forest.' This forestry walk is similar to the earlier one but on a grander scale—you could spend half a day here if you have the time and interest. Write-ups explain logging practices and reforestation procedures.

You come to a T intersection with the Ucluelet-Tofino Highway at kilometre 47 (mile 29). Turn left to visit Albion and Ucluelet.

## Plants of Vancouver Island's West Coast

The Japanese Current is warm water that crosses the North Pacific Ocean from Asia to the west coast of the North American continent. This current creates a moist and moderate climate along the western slopes of the mountains and causes heavy precipitation. The coastal lowlands support lush rainforests of hemlock, redcedar, yellow-cedar and balsam fir. In valleys and on higher slopes, giant cedars and Douglas-fir reach heights in the range of 60 metres (200 feet). In these damper areas, which receive between 1500 and 2500 millimetres (60 and 100 inches) of precipitation annually, there is an abundance of ferns and shrubs such as salal, salmonberry and devil's club. In contrast, the drier rain-shadow climate towards the southeastern corner of the island better supports maples, Garry oak and arbutus.

## PORT ALBION & UCLUELET

In 1.2 kilometres (0.7 mile) you reach the side road to the village of Port Albion. It was established by European settlers in the 1880s, beside an already-existing Native village near the entrance to the Ucluelet Inlet. When more settlers arrived,

Canadian Princess, *Ucluelet*

they found that land was cheaper on the other side of the inlet and so they moved to what became the town of Ucluelet. Today Port Albion is a Native village.

Continue down the main road and 5 kilometres (3 miles) from the road to Port Albion you reach Ucluelet, which was a prehistoric fishing port. The name comes from the Native name Yu-clutl-ahts, meaning 'the people with a good landing place for canoes' or 'safe harbour.' It is set on the eastern side of the strip of land that forms the western side of Ucluelet Inlet, near its southern tip. While sheltered from the storms of the Pacific, it is nevertheless close to the feeding grounds of the migrating salmon. The village bills itself as 'the Whale Watching Capital.'

As you drive through town on Peninsula Road, watch on your left for the huge, bright white, 70-metre (230-foot) *Canadian Princess* moored at the dock. Permanently anchored here, this historic steamship has been turned into a floating hotel with staterooms, dining room, lounge and bar. Smaller ships tie up alongside her and then leave to take passengers out to Barkley Sound and other destinations. There is plenty of parking here if you wish to stop and have lunch aboard.

## The *Canadian Princess*

*When the* Canadian Princess *was built, she was known as the* William J. Stewart. *As a Canadian Hydrographic Service ship, she charted the BC coast from 1934 to 1975. In 1944, she struck Ripple Rock in Seymour Narrows (see Chapter 11). It took months to fix the extensive damage and refloat her. In 1975 she sailed for the last time, arriving in Victoria in September. She was bought by new owners in 1979 and refurbished into a floating hotel. With her name changed and a new function, she was towed to Ucluelet Harbour.*

Throughout Ucluelet there are a number of restaurants that serve fresh shrimp, and also galleries and gift shops. To reach Amphitrite Point and a lighthouse, continue about 1 kilometre (0.6 mile) south of the village and turn right onto Coast Guard Drive. In about one-half kilometre (0.3 mile) you come to a parking lot beside the lighthouse.

*Lighthouse, Ucluelet*

The lighthouse, which was built in 1905, is at the southern tip of the Ucluth Peninsula, which juts out from the end of the Ucluelet Peninsula. From here you can see 'the Ship's Graveyard,' so-called because of all the ships that have run aground here, at the entrance to Barkley Sound. In the building beside the lighthouse the Canadian Coast Guard operates a marine communications and vessel traffic service to keep ships informed of other activity in the area.

As you stand at the point, listen for a sound something like a foghorn. It is actually the whistle-buoy that marks Carolina Channel at the entrance to Ucluelet Inlet. The ocean waves compress the air in the buoy, triggering the whistle. The noise alerts mariners to the edge of the shipping channel.

## PACIFIC RIM NATIONAL PARK

Return to the T intersection where you first came down to the Ucluelet-Tofino Highway and go straight to head towards Tofino. In 1 kilometre (0.6 mile) you enter Pacific Rim National Park and just past the entrance you cross the 49th Parallel. This is the only road that goes through the park to Tofino. Signs along the way indicate side roads and hiking trails.

*Wickaninnish, Long Beach*

If you want to stop anywhere in the park, buy a pass (for a day or a week) from one of the vending machines located in a parking area. When you park your vehicle, display your pass on your dash so that wardens can see it. (Note: At this writing, the cost for a day pass is $5 and the machines only take $5 bills, so plan ahead.)

Watch for the road to the left to the Wickaninnish Centre overlooking Wickaninnish Beach. This wheelchair-accessible facility uses models, displays and films to promote a better understanding of the largest and deepest body of water on earth, the Pacific Ocean. The Pacific, by the way, was given its name in 1513 by Spanish explorer Balboa, who was impressed by its calm and peaceful appearance when he first saw it. Among the displays are a whaling canoe and whale bones. There is also a restaurant where you can enjoy your meal while watching the Pacific Ocean lapping at the beach.

| **Pacific Rim National Park** | *Pacific Rim National* |
| --- | --- |

*Park includes over 500 square kilometres (190 square miles) of land and consists of three parts: Long Beach and area, the Broken Group Islands and the West Coast Trail (see Chapters 2 and 3). Each section is separated from the others by water and has its own access points.*

*Long Beach is at the end of the Pacific Rim Highway from Port Alberni. The Broken Group Islands comprises over one hundred islets and islands and is reachable by water only. The West Coast Trail has its terminuses at Bamfield and Port Renfrew. It is 77 kilometres (48 miles) long and can only be travelled by hikers (see Chapter 2). An unusual feature of the park is that its border extends into the Pacific Ocean, thus protecting giant kelp, octopi and the rest of the marine environment out to where the water reaches a depth of 18 metres (10 fathoms or 60 feet).*

As you drive the Wickaninnish Road, stop to walk the Shorepine Bog Trail, from which you can see stunted and twisted trees that are hundreds of years old. As a contrast to the bog, take a walk through a rainforest.

To get to the Rainforest Trail, get back onto the highway and head northwest for about 4 kilometres (2.5 miles) until you come to the parking area at the trailhead. The trail is made up of two loops, one on each side of the highway. Each loop is about 1.2 kilometres (0.7 mile) long. The rainforest includes eight-hundred-year-old western redcedars, three-hundred-year-old hemlocks and also amabalis firs that are hundreds of years old. Because of the wet climate, this forest has not been touched by natural fire.

*Ramp at Long Beach*

To get to Long Beach, drive a few minutes more along the highway, past Green Point, to the turn-off into the Long Beach parking lot. The beach is truly very long and very wide when the tide is out. Stroll along the sand and watch the surf come in. It can be a surprising experience to find that you do not leave footprints in the hard-packed sand. Even the little ripples in the sand do not flatten out when you

**Rip Currents** *While ocean waves usually hit the shore straight on, in some places currents occur that run parallel to the shore. When these currents come into contact with rock formations, they can turn and head right out to sea, becoming what are known as 'rip currents.' If you are swimming and get caught in a rip current, you might not be able to make it back to land, no matter how strong a swimmer you are. (If you do get caught, swim perpendicular to the current, rather than tire yourself out trying to fight it, until you get out of it and can swim back to shore.)*

*These currents are bad at Wickaninnish and Green Point and near the huge rock that you see straight out from the Long Beach parking lot. Also, if you go swimming at Florencia Bay, south of Wickaninnish Beach, do not swim near either end of the beach there.*

step on them. The compacted sand moves only when you work at it, such as by scraping it with your heel.

Long Beach is 'the Surfing Capital of Canada.' Especially in winter, its huge breakers rival those of California. While the surfboards used here are the same, the lower water temperatures mean that most surfers wear wet suits or dry suits—although some hardy souls do ride the waves wearing just their swimsuits. Surfers, windsurfers and kayakers sometimes hold competitions here. If you do not have any gear, you can rent some in Tofino.

About seventeen thousand Pacific gray whales swim past Long Beach on their annual ten-thousand-kilometre (six-thousand-mile) spring migration from California to Alaska between February and May. Grays are the only species of whale that migrates close enough to the shore to be seen from land. Watch for the 5-metre (16-foot) high blasts from their blowholes. On their way southwards in the fall, they travel farther out from land and are not as visible. Tofino and Ucluelet hold an annual Pacific Rim Whale Festival from mid-March to mid-April, when the migration is at its peak.

If you are a birdwatcher, note that 250 different species of birds have been seen in Pacific Rim National Park, 49 of which nest here in the spring.

If you enjoy the power and fury of winter storms, Long Beach is the place for you. The storms swirl down from the Bering Sea and the Gulf of Alaska, creating 100-kilometre-per-hour (60-mile-per-hour) winds with gusts to 130 kilometres per hour (80 miles per hour). The storms move counter-clockwise as they churn southwards and hit the west coast of Vancouver Island from the southwest. They have dumped as much as 1613 millimetres (63.5 inches) of rain on the area between November and February. Once the winds have subsided, there is a treasure trove of articles

*Surfers, Long Beach*

on the beach that have been raised from the deep, washed off ships or drifted in from some exotic place. Beachcombing can be a profitable excursion after a storm.

The naturalists at Pacific Rim National Park offer talks and guided tours of the area. Evening programs take place at the 230-seat theatre in the Green Point Campground.

On your way to Tofino, watch for the turn-off on your left for Radar Hill, named for a former military installation. You drive through an archway of branches and it is calming and cool in the mostly total shade as you follow the 1.2-kilometre (0.7-mile) road up the hill to the parking lot. There is a wheelchair-accessible viewing platform that overlooks Clayoquot Sound, the islands off the shore and the trees below.

## TOFINO

Back on the road to Tofino, you leave Pacific Rim National Park just after the road to Radar Hill. There are resorts, adventure tour companies and restaurants on the way into Tofino.

Tofino is a fishing village on the southern edge of Clayoquot Sound. It began as a Clayoquot Native village and was one of the places visited by Captain Cook in 1778.

You come into the village on Campbell Street. If you want to see where the crab pots (traps) are stored, look for Olsen Street on your right and turn onto it to go to the crab dock. To watch fresh fish being unloaded from fishboats, go to Fishermen's Wharf on Fourth Street or the government wharf on First Street. The restaurants in the village offer a variety of fresh seafood.

There are two art galleries on Campbell Street: Eagle Aerie and Schooner galleries are on opposite sides of Campbell at Second Street.

Take a whale-watching cruise or rent a boat to go fishing or diving. Cruises are offered from the government wharf to Hot

Crab dock, Tofino

Springs Cove, the only hot springs on Vancouver Island. From where the boat or seaplane drops you off, it is a 30-minute hike through the rainforest to reach the site.

There is the usual smell of sulphur as you near the six pools fed by the warm waters. The water of the first one can reach 50 degrees Celsius (122 degrees Fahrenheit) and as the water flows to the other pools, it loses temperature. The last pool is fed by ocean water, a nice cool change from the hot springs. Many people believe that these pools help relieve arthritis and rheumatism.

Since Tofino is at the very end of the road, when you are done here, you need to retrace your path back up Highway 4 before you can drive anywhere else.

# CHAPTER 7

# LASQUETI ISLAND to SHELTER BAY

*Most of the villages along this part of Highway 19 seem to blend together and it is hard to tell when you leave one and enter another. As you head northwards, watch to your left for the snowcapped mountains down the centre of Vancouver Island. On this route you will visit some historic sites and towns and be able to take ferries to three Northern Gulf Islands. Because the islands are small and you can hardly get lost, no distance measurements are given. The atmosphere is more relaxed than in the city, so do not hurry through them.*

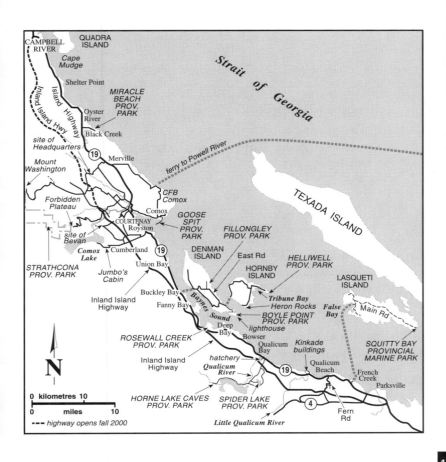

## LASQUETI ISLAND

To begin this route, drive up the Island Highway (Highway 19) to the northwest from Nanaimo, past the intersection with Highway 4, to Parksville. (If you are on Highway 4 coming from Port Alberni, take the Parksville turn-off and turn left onto Highway 19.) Drive northwards through Parksville to the settlement of French Creek. Then watch for the road to the right that leads to the ferry dock.

When planning your trip to Lasqueti Island, bear in mind that the ferry runs just two or three times each day, with no trips on Tuesdays in the summer and on neither Tuesdays nor Wednesdays in the winter. Also, you will have to leave your car on Vancouver Island, because the ferry takes foot passengers only, though for a small fee you can bring a bicycle, canoe, kayak, your dog or a few boxes of freight.

You arrive at False Bay after about a 50-minute ride. If you would rather not go on foot as you explore the island, at the bay you can rent a bicycle (but do be careful riding the island's gravel roads—not recommended for beginner cyclists).

Lasqueti Island is 21 kilometres (13 miles) long and about 5 kilometres (3 miles) wide. Though there are roads, there is not much traffic because residents have to hire a barge if they want to get a car or truck over to the island, and the same is true for other kinds of large freight. Many residents of Lasqueti keep a vehicle at False Bay and another one at French Creek. While Lasqueti has residential phone service, it does not have electrical power distributed to its homes. Residents who want electricity make their own using solar energy, windmills, water-driven turbines or gasoline-powered generators.

Over the years, settlers have tried to make a living logging, farming, raising sheep and cattle, mining, growing winterberry and salal for sale to florists and fishing. The successful crops now are garlic and fruit trees, with some oyster- and clam-farming.

If you wish to spend the night on the island, there is a hotel at False Bay and there is a bed-and-breakfast as well. There are no public rest rooms on Lasqueti and the only pit toilets are at Squitty Bay Provincial Marine Park, at the far end of the island from the ferry dock.

If you wish to see some of the island, you will have to walk along the unpaved roads—or bicycle, or befriend an islander with a vehicle. There are some hiking trails on the island but they are through private land and you must ask permission to use them. While you are here, you can visit the small shopping area along Main Road (right at the dock and scattered for about 1.5 kilometres (1 mile) up the road) or rent a boat at the dock to tour around the shoreline.

## QUALICUM BEACH & QUALICUM BAY

Qualicum Beach calls itself 'the Most Popular Summer Getaway on the Island.' Being popular usually means being busy and crowded, and Qualicum Beach is both.

But if you can handle the congestion, find a parking spot and walk out onto the beach. There is a seawall along the beach for quite a ways and anywhere along here you can park and walk on the seawall or play in the sand. The beach is really a lovely place. In the early morning, when it is cool and peaceful, it is at its best and there are only a few birds and joggers to disturb your solitude. Look across the strait to see the mountains of the mainland.

While in Qualicum Beach, visit the Old Schoolhouse Gallery and Art Centre in the restored 1914 schoolhouse. To get there, turn left onto Memorial Avenue, follow it one block past 2nd Avenue and turn right onto Fern Road. The centre is at 122 Fern Road West. There is a wide variety of arts and crafts to see in the two galleries, with a number of studios fitted with viewing windows through which you can watch the artists do their work.

Continue along Highway 19 through town. Just out of Qualicum Beach, after the seawall and the parking ends, watch for Kinkade Road. Turn right onto it and in less than one-half kilometre (about 0.25 mile) there is a curve to the left and the road becomes McFeely Drive. If you look to your left as you drive along, you can see the faded old Kinkade house and barn out in the bush and high grass by themselves.

This house was built by Thomas Kinkade in 1885. He and his family moved here in 1884 and lived on a sloop while he constructed the house from hand-hewn logs. He also erected two dykes using just a shovel and a wheelbarrow. On their property the Kinkades discovered remnants of a large stockade and some human skeletons. When asked

*Seawall, Qualicum Beach*

about it, some visiting Natives told them that many of the people who had lived here had died from smallpox and the ones who survived the disease had set fire to the stockade before leaving.

This property is adjacent to the estuary of the Little Qualicum River and the fenced area around the house and barn is a national wildlife preserve. If you are a birdwatcher, take note that 215 different species of birds have been sighted in the region.

For another look at the historic buildings, continue on McFeely Drive to Surfside Drive. Turn left, drive past the row of houses and look to your left when you come to the fence again. (Note that the property is not open to the public.)

Back on Highway 19, you soon cross the Little Qualicum River. Natives used to set traps to catch the salmon on this river in the fall. They set up camp and for weeks smoked thousands of fish for their winter food. The Little Qualicum is still one of the best fishing streams on the island.

In 13.3 kilometres (8.3 miles) from the Little Qualicum River, you reach Horne Lake Road. It goes not only to Horne Lake but also to Spider Lake Provincial Park and Horne Lake Caves Provincial Park. Just down the road, make a right at the T intersection. Then, just after you cross the Inland Island Highway, look on the left for the entrance for Spider Lake Provincial Park. At Spider Lake you can fish for black bass, but note that no power boats are allowed on the lake.

After Spider Lake, the road curves to the right and in 10.2 kilometres (6.3 miles) from Highway 19, you pass a logging road on your right that leads back to the highway. Keep left here and you can see Horne Lake on your left.

Horne Lake Caves Provincial Park is at the end of the lake. Park in the parking lot and follow the trail over a suspension bridge spanning the Qualicum River to the caves.

Two smaller caves, Lower and Main, are open to the public for self-guiding tours. Even with their narrow passageways and the vandalism that has occurred, they are still enjoyable to climb through. Main Cave has a waterfall just past the entrance. If you intend to explore these caves, carry two sources of light, make sure that your arms and legs are covered and wear rubber-soled shoes. These caves are not suitable for children under the age of five, who are too small.

Riverbend Cave is larger than the others, but is open only for guided tours. These 1.5-hour tours are good for families, though they may be a bit much for children under five. The passages in this cave are wider than in the other caves and the beautiful crystal formations are undamaged. All necessary equipment is supplied with the price of the tour.

For more information on the Horne Lake Caves, call 250-757-8687.

Back on Highway 19, in just 0.5 kilometre (0.3 mile) from Horne Lake Road, you reach the turnoff for the Big Qualicum River Fish Hatchery, which is only 0.8 kilometre (0.5 mile) off the highway.

Typically, out of every 750 salmon eggs laid in the wild, only one fish survives to come back and spawn. This government-run hatchery aims to improve the odds by controlling factors such as water temperature and flow rate, in what is said to be the world's first environmental control program for salmon propagation.

The water for the hatchery comes from Horne Lake. The three intake pipes are at different water levels to take advantage of the different temperatures at each level. Valves located at the gate shaft house on the lake control the speed of the water.

Visit the hatchery in the fall if you want to see the salmon return to spawn—or you can stop in at any time during the day in spring and summer to see the facilities.

Return to Highway 19 and turn left. You cross the (Big) Qualicum River and enter Qualicum Bay, a resort town with motels, parking for recreational vehicles, crafts for sale and various shops. Then continue up the highway to the town of Bowser.

## BOWSER & FANNY BAY

Bowser, which overlooks the ocean, was named for a former premier of British Columbia, William John Bowser. In the late 1930s, a dog named Mike worked as a bartender in the Bowser Hotel. He would carry the bottles of beer to the customers, pick up their money and take it to the bar, and then return with the change. His feats got him into Ripley's Believe It Or Not. He died in 1941 and the Bowser Hotel, which had been built in 1925, was destroyed by fire in 1969.

There are a number of bays after Bowser that offer fishing and RV parking. Stop at any of them if you wish to camp or fish or rest awhile.

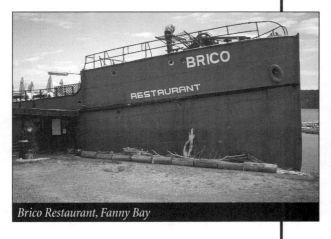

Past Deep Bay, but before you cross Rosewall Creek, you can turn right onto Berray Road to stop in at Rosewall Creek Provincial Park. You can walk through the park and across the creek on bridges and paths that are wide enough for wheelchairs. It is a lovely spot on a warm day.

*Brico Restaurant, Fanny Bay*

Island Sun Greenhouses are to your left just as you come into Fanny Bay. You can stop in to buy plants for your garden or some flowers for your camper if the spirit moves you.

The settlement of Fanny Bay is a leftover from early logging in the area. As you drive along the shore of Fanny Bay, you pass a big, blue hotel and then a large, red ship settled in the sand. The ship houses the Brico Restaurant. On its deck there are tables with umbrellas for you to sit at and enjoy the view out over the ocean as you eat your lunch. The restaurant, which opens at noon, offers lunch and dinner specials and a variety of seafood.

## DENMAN ISLAND

At Buckley Bay, 2 kilometres (1.2 miles) past the Brico Restaurant, turn right for the Denman Island Ferry. There are nearly twenty sailings per day in each direction and the trip takes 10–15 minutes. When you pay for your ferry tickets, tell the clerk if you plan to continue on to Hornby Island, and, if you have not already picked one up at a tourist information centre, ask for a map of the islands.

Denman Island is separated from Vancouver Island by Baynes Sound. It is 19 kilometres (12 miles) long and about 6 kilometres (4 miles) wide. It has two small lakes and two even smaller ones. There are few bays or coves and it is relatively flat. It is not as popular with tourists as its neighbour, Hornby Island.

## Some Notes to Remember

*If you see signs on the beaches of the islands that indicate oyster or clam leases, stay off them, especially below the normal high-tide line. Walking on them could damage the oysters, which live on top of the sand and are quite fragile when young and tiny. Young clams are also easily injured.*

*Camp only in designated areas and check to make sure that camp-fires are permitted before you light one.*

*Water on Denman and Hornby is scarce during the summer and fall so use it sparingly or bring your own.*

*There is no garbage pick-up on the islands, so please take your trash with you.*

The first non-Native settlers were from the Orkney Islands, located off the northern end of Scotland. The immigrants opened a sandstone quarry in 1908 and worked it for seven years. Agriculture and dairy farming became popular and the first fall fair was held on the island in 1916. Logging, which had begun in the early 1900s, ended in 1950 when most of the island had been logged. Oyster farming is a big industry now and most of the western shore has oyster farms.

Once you get off the ferry, the road curves to the right and goes over a speed bump. Look to your left here for a sign that reads, 'Denman Island' and has flowers under it. A plaque dedicates the site to the memory of Harold G. Walton (February 2, 1906 to August 15, 1988) who used to look after the flowers.

To the left of the sign there is an anchor from the *SS Alpha*, which went down near Chrome Island (off the southern tip of Denman) on December 20, 1900. The anchor was found on October 22, 1972.

You are on Denman Road when you leave the ferry. The island's general store and a small business centre are to the left when you reach the junction at the top of the climb up from the ferry. Keep right at this junction and then curve left to stay on Denman Road. Once you get away from the business centre, most of the driving is along tree-lined country roads. There are residences along many of the island's roads, but they are often hidden by trees.

As you continue on Denman Road, you pass the Denman Island Old School Centre on your right. The brown building contains the Islands Trust office, workshops for spinners and weavers and the recycling centre.

*Denman Island*

To visit Fillongley Provincial Park, turn left off Denman Road onto Swan Road, right on Beadnell Road and go to the parking lot at the end of the road. This park, which offers many short hiking trails, was originally the estate of George Beadnell. His parents had bought the land in 1889 and gave it the name 'Fillongley,' from their home in Warwick, England.

When George took over the land, he and his wife, Amy, built a lily pond, benches, bridges and birdhouses. They planted trees and laid out flower-beds, a bowling green and paths through the forest. By the time they were finished, it was a beautiful parklike setting. George wanted to deed his land to the government when he died, but under BC law he could not, so in 1953 he sold it to the government—for one dollar.

Past Swan Road, Denman Road curves right and becomes East Road. As you drive along here you can see Hornby Island to your left. There are several orchards on this road if you want to buy fresh apples, pears, or plums in season.

Instead of turning left onto Gravelly Bay Road to take the Hornby Island Ferry, go straight ahead onto the gravel road and you soon reach Boyle Point Provincial Park. The road ends at the parking lot and the hiking trails start from here. One will take you to a steep cliff from which you can see Chrome Island and the Chrome Island Light Station. The lighthouse you see was built in 1898, the second one on the island. The first lighthouse was constructed in 1891, on the opposite side of the island.

Another trail will take you to a different cliff above the ocean from which you can see Eagle Rock. While it is possible to work your way down the embankment and out to the rock at very low tide, keep an eye on the water so that you do not get stranded. Camping is not permitted in the park.

## HORNBY ISLAND

Hornby Island is reached by a 10-minute ferry ride from Gravelly Bay, towards the southeastern end of Denman Island. As you cross, notice Mount Geoffrey, the highest point on this small island, which is about 3.5 kilometres (2 miles) long and 2.5 kilometres (1.5 miles) wide.

Non-Natives had settled across most of Hornby by 1900, although the population was only about thirty people. They supported themselves by fishing, farming and logging. Much of the original forest on the island was logged by 1920.

There is no public campground but there are a few private campsites and many bed-and-breakfasts. Most of

*Heron Rocks, Hornby Island*

the services are near Tribune Bay, on the east side of the island.

As you get off the ferry on Hornby, look to your left to see the Hornby Island Resort Pub. Because of the dried grass on its roof, it is also called 'the Thatched Pub.' Watch for other buildings with thatched or sod roofs on the island.

*Heron Rocks*

As you leave the ferry, you are on Shingle Spit Road. When the road makes a sharp curve to the right, it becomes Central Road. There are signs up all along the island's roads for galleries, studios and artists. If you are interested, stop in and look at their work.

You reach a four-way stop at the Co-op Store near Tribune Bay. The road to Helliwell Park is to the left. Since you will come back this way anyway, for now follow Central Road as it turns right here and eventually passes Strachan Road on the right. Soon you come to a sign on the left that reads, 'Heron Rocks Co-op and Friendship Centre,' and another one that has 'Heron Rocks' etched into it. Turn left off the road onto a small gravel track. You are in a tall forest where the trees are close to the road and the branches hang low. Then you reach a small parking lot with a sign stating that it is private property.

Walk down the private road to the house. You have to ask permission to walk out to the rocks here; at the same time, inquire about the tides. There is a small tenting campsite on the beach. Only registered campers can drive into the campground and then only to unload their equipment and then again to pack up when it is time to leave.

Stroll through the small area and out to the beach to get to the rocks. It is like stepping onto another planet or entering a science-fiction movie—the sight is really unbelievable. Some of the rocks have hollows containing pools of water left in them by the last high tide. Others have been worn into unusual shapes. As you walk amongst the rocks, watch for damp spots and slippery vegetation. Make sure that you have plenty of film and lots of time to spend, because each rock formation is amazing.

If you prefer, you can drive a little farther, to the end of Central Road, and park at Ford's Cove, a more public place, and walk back to Heron Rocks at low tide from there.

Go back on Central Road towards the four-way stop sign. Stop in at the service station, Co-op Store or craft market if you like and then go straight ahead. The entrance to Tribune Bay Provincial Park, with its wonderful beaches, is to the right. Then, continue on to St. John's Point Road and turn right to head for Helliwell Provincial Park. On the way you pass the north side of Tribune Bay Park on your right and

**Moonshine at Heron Rocks** *During Prohibition, one of Hornby's farmers was a Chinese immigrant named Yick Shing. He had a farm near Heron Rocks where he grew vegetables to be shipped to market in Nanaimo. Because he had a number of Chinese workers on his farm, he imported large amounts of rice from his homeland to feed his workers—or so he told everyone. Actually, he was using most of the rice to make whisky, which he produced with a still hidden in his barn. He then bottled the moonshine and packed the bottles in sauerkraut in waterproof boxes. These boxes were then concealed under the vegetables heading to market.*

*When he was caught, he received a three-year prison sentence. A frequent visitor to the jail to see Yick was his cousin. Knowing that the European jailers had a hard time telling Chinese men apart, Yick and his cousin would change clothes on the visits and Yick would leave the jail disguised as his cousin. When the 'cousin' returned for another visit, they would swap clothes again and Yick would remain in the jail. With the help of his cousin, he thus avoided having to serve his full sentence himself.*

then begin to pass, on your left, Whaling Station Bay, which was used by the Comox Natives as a fishing camp long before Europeans began to use it as a whaling station in 1871. Take the right branch at the fork to reach Helliwell Provincial Park at the end of the road. There is no drinking water in the park, so bring your own.

A loop trail begins at the Helliwell parking lot. A small cairn at the trailhead recognizes the generosity of Mr. John Helliwell in donating the land for this park. The trail is about 5 kilometres (3 miles) long and takes about one and one-half hours to walk. The trail takes you through an old-growth forest of Douglas-fir and red-cedar, beside the waters of the Strait of Georgia and along the unusual black cliffs for which Helliwell is known.

Drive back the way you came, turning right at the four-way stop at the Co-op Store to follow Central Road back to the ferry.

## UNION BAY & ROYSTON

After you leave the ferry terminal and continue up the Island Highway, you pass through some more of Buckley Bay—mainly resorts and houses. In 2 kilometres (1.2 miles), however, you have the ocean and beach immediately to your right.

If you would like to picnic right next to the ocean, you can pull over at the Baynes Sound Rest Area, marked by the sign that welcomes you to Union Bay. The beach is quite rocky, so it is not the easiest for walking. Notice the commercial oyster fishing lease here, marked by the buoys bobbing on the water's surface. The oysters are sold to restaurants and shops in the area.

From this rest stop you can look out at the Strait of Georgia, Denman and Texada islands and the mountains on the mainland. As you continue driving towards Union Bay, you can still enjoy the sight of the ocean to your right.

The settlement of Union Bay was built in 1889 as the seaport for the Union Coal Mining Company, which had mines near Cumberland. Robert Dunsmuir had bought all the coal-rich land in the area in the early 1880s and had chosen this site because of its deep waters. The coal was transported over the 19 kilometres (12 miles) of track from Cumberland to the waiting ships at Union Bay. The Union Bay wharf was one of the longest on the island. The tracks continued out onto it so that the rail-cars of coal could be loaded directly onto the ocean-going ships. (There will be more on Cumberland and the mines shortly.)

There is a large area for parking by the water if you wish to tour the town of Union Bay or walk out onto the rock wharf. A sign by the parking lot tells about Albert 'Ginger' Goodwin, who took part in the 1912-14 mineworkers' strike on the island—the Cumberland part of the New Inland Island Highway was designated 'the Ginger Goodwin Way.'

After Union Bay you can see the ocean only occasionally. You cross the Trent River, where coal was discovered in 1869, and reach Royston. Royston is on the hills overlooking the Comox Harbour. When you come into Royston, watch for the left turn to Cumberland.

# CUMBERLAND

It is a nice drive beside acreages and beautiful yards as you follow Royston Road to the Village of Cumberland. You reach the welcome sign and an ore car at 4.5 kilometres (2.8 miles) from Royston, but you are still some distance from downtown.

Sightings of coal in the area were made in the early 1850s and again in the 1860s. In 1869, a Native brought some miners from Nanaimo to the region and showed them the black rock seams along what is now Coal Creek. The miners formed the Union Coal Mining Company and a town, Union, grew up nearby to supply the mines. They began taking the coal out, but before they could build railway tracks to Royston to move it to the ocean to be shipped off and sold, they ran out of money.

Robert Dunsmuir bought up the claims and built a road from Royston to Union. He and his son, James, then tried to build a rail terminal on Comox Harbour at Royston but land prices were too high, so in 1889 they instead built it at what became Union Bay. Robert Dunsmuir is the one who renamed the village of Union in honor of the English county from which of many of the miners came—Cumberland.

Over the following years, a total of seven mines operated in the area, but by 1955 most of the mining had ended, with only a few small workings left. They folded in 1967. Over their years of operation, more than 260 men were killed in accidents in the Cumberland mines.

Cumberland, in the foothills of the Beaufort Mountains, is now a historic village. The road you come into town on is Dunsmuir Avenue. Go down this street to see the historic buildings, which have been kept in good shape. Notice that the houses are square. The old custom-house and post office, a large brick building dating from 1907, is on the corner of Dunsmuir and Third.

Part-way down the street you come to a row of six colourfully painted two-storey buildings all joined together as one. While each business has its own distinctive front, there is a walkway that joins all the top storeys. Each of the six still bears on its top storey the name of its original business: 'Sunon Wo Com. Merchandise 1927,' 'Miners' Recreation Hall,' 'Canadian Collieries Office,' etc. At the end of this row there is a one-storey building that houses the Cumberland Museum.

Cumberland's Chinatown began with 150 men in 1888. Over the next forty years, as more men immigrated from China or moved from other places in the province to find

## Comox Valley

The Comox Valley is centred around the Comox River, near the middle of the eastern side of Vancouver Island. Its main communities are the Village of Cumberland, the Town of Comox and the City of Courtenay.

When non-Natives began to settle here in 1862, the valley had long since been home to the Comox Natives. While the Natives fished off the shores, the newcomers farmed the land.

Temperatures here are mild, with July being the hottest and driest month. In July, the average daytime temperature is 23 degrees Celsius (73 degrees Fahrenheit) and the average rainfall for the month is only 28 millimetres (1.1 inches).

The valley is the winter home for many birds, the most spectacular of which is the trumpeter swan. This species returns here every November and leaves again in March.

*Sign at Cumberland*

work, their numbers increased to a high of three thousand in the late 1920s. During its heyday, Cumberland's Chinatown was the second largest Chinese community outside China, next to San Francisco's Chinatown.

To see where Cumberland's Chinatown was, drive through town until you reach Sutton Street on the left, which goes to Comox Lake. Turn onto it and follow it as it curves to the right in just over one block from Dunsmuir. In a few minutes you reach a stop of interest and 'Jumbo's Cabin.'

Originally built as a jail, this cabin was taken over by the Union Colliery Company from 1869 to 1883 and became their office. It later ended up as the home of Mar Hor Shui, the last resident of Cumberland's Chinatown, who lived there until 1971.

When the mines closed, the workers moved away to seek other jobs. Many of the town's deserted buildings were destroyed in a fire in 1968—only Jumbo's Cabin remains.

Continue along this road and just past the cabin there is a cairn that marks the spot where Cumberland's black community lived between 1893 and 1960. Another cairn

## The Chinese Workers

*In the 1800s, thousands of Chinese workers fled the poverty and civil war in China. Many came to British Columbia to pursue the gold rushes. They usually reworked areas that had already been mined by the white miners.*

*They also helped to build the railways or worked on other construction projects or found employment in white men's mines. They were generally paid less than white workers and treated poorly. For support and security, the Chinese workers began to gather together. Their little towns of cabins or shacks and became known as 'Chinatowns.'*

less than one-half kilometre (0.3 mile) down the road is for the Number 4 Mine, which operated from 1890 to 1935. Between 1922 and 1923, 51 miners died in explosions in this mine.

To see the remains of a coal town, go back into Cumberland and turn left onto Fourth Street. After the road curves to the right, watch for Bevan Street and turn left onto it. Paved for the first while, it turns to gravel. In 6.4 kilometres (4 miles) you come to a stop sign. Go straight and in less than 1 kilometre (0.5 mile) you reach North Comox Lake Hostel, which caters to hikers and cyclists who are touring the area.

The hostel is beside the former site of Bevan, a coal town built in 1911. As you drive into the yard, there is a fence to your left. On the other side you can see the old foundations that remain where the Bevan Hotel and other buildings once stood.

*Cumberland*

## COURTENAY

There are several ways to Courtenay from the North Comox Lake Hostel. If you are in a hurry, the quicker route is to drive out of the yard and turn left. Continue along the road that goes past the hostel, which from here on is paved and is called Lake Trail Road. In 4.3 kilometres (2.7 miles) you come to a stop sign. Turn left here and you soon enter the outskirts of Courtenay. Continue until you reach a T intersection, where you turn right onto Piercy Road. In one block you reach Cumberland Road. Turn left and drive to a set of traffic lights. Go through them, now on 8th Street, and in two blocks you reach Cliffe Avenue (formerly part of Highway 19) in downtown Courtenay.

Two other ways involve returning to Cumberland first. From there, one option is to turn left when you get to the end of Bevan Street and then turn left again onto Cumberland Road and follow it into Courtenay and proceed as above. However, you could also take Royston Road back to the Island Highway, turn left and follow it into Courtenay. If you drive into Courtenay along this last route, you will pass the 'Mile of Flowers,' which begins at 29th Street. Each spring the

*Courtney Hotel*

*Courtney Museum*

community plants brightly coloured flowers along the boulevard of this stretch of highway for residents and tourists to enjoy.

Courtenay was named after Rear Admiral George William Courtenay. He was the captain of the *HMS Constance*, which sailed up and down the coast between 1845 and 1849. He was also in charge of the first surveying expedition in the area.

If you come into town on Highway 19, look for the tourist information booth on the right shortly after you pass 26th Street. In the yard there are a totem pole and an old steam engine. The engine used to pull a train that hauled logs to Union Bay. It has been restored, including a brass bell. You can climb up and look inside.

To see 'the largest free-span log structure in Canada,' follow the signs for the museum, which is located in the Native Sons of Canada Hall. When the highway curves to the right at 17th Street, go straight ahead to 360 Cliffe Avenue.

The Native Sons of Canada, a group of Canadian-born Caucasians, constructed the building as a community hall for Courtenay in 1928. The walls are made of five hundred upright cedar logs. There are no supports inside—it is the strength and size of the logs that keep the building standing.

All of the museum's displays are on the main floor; the upstairs is currently being used for storage. Along with historic artifacts, there is a scale model of a Native longhouse. Also look for the replica of the elasmosaur, a marine reptile, whose remains were discovered along the Puntledge River in 1988. The elasmosaur died out with the other dinosaurs about 65 million years ago.

If you want to visit Lewis Park, which is on the river bank, go northwards on Cliffe Avenue to 5th Street. Turn right onto the Old Island Highway to cross the Courtenay River and look to your left—the park has a totem pole on each side of its entrance. On your right, across the road from the park, is the Courtenay House Hotel, built in the late 1880s.

Return on Cliffe Avenue to 17th Street and turn left onto Highway 19 to immediately cross the Courtenay River, which is claimed to be the shortest tidal river in the world.

# COMOX

Right after the bridge, turn right onto Comox Road, which was sometimes called 'Dyke Road' on old maps because it was built on a dyke. When you reach town it becomes Comox Avenue.

Comox was originally called 'Komuckway' after the Native band that already lived here. Over the years, settlers changed the spelling of the word, which means 'plenty,' to 'Komoux' and then to 'Comox.'

To go to the provincial park at Goose Spit, drive through town (the route in this chapter takes you back this way afterwards) to Pritchard Road and turn left. Just after getting onto Pritchard, you reach a four-way stop. Turn right onto Balmoral Avenue and when Balmoral ends, continue straight on Hawkins Road. Stay on Hawkins to go to Goose Spit Provincial Park.

This spit was used for centuries by the Comox and Puntlatch Native groups as a site to camp. At low tide you can lie on the sand and look at the mountains, have a picnic or walk on the sandy spit, which juts out into the blue waters of Comox Harbour.

Return to the junction of Comox Avenue and Pritchard Road and turn left onto Comox. Then turn in at the entrance for the Filberg Lodge and Park on the right.

The Filberg Heritage Lodge and Park is on 3.6 hectares (8.9 acres) overlooking Comox Harbour. The construction of the lodge began in 1929 and the Filberg family lived there for many years. When Mr. Robert Filberg died in 1977, he donated the home to the Vancouver Foundation. With help from different levels of government and donations from private individuals and companies, the grounds were developed into a heritage park.

Besides the lodge, which has a stone fireplace and is open to tour, there are the gardens with their many rare plants and trees, a herb garden, the tea house and an animal farm for the children. The annual strawberry tea takes place here at the end of June and the Filberg Festival is held in the beginning of August. As many as 140 artists appear at the festival and set up their booths under the tall trees. You can wander from booth to booth admiring or buying arts and crafts, listening to the live entertainment and sampling some gourmet cooking.

Through providing a venue for the artists to display and sell their work, the festival encourages them to excel at their arts and crafts. The event also gives the public a chance to see some exceptional work and to meet the people behind it.

If you are interested in aviation, go to Canadian Forces Base Comox, where there is a museum with displays that recount the history of Canada's Air Force—from the first flight of the *Silver Dart* to modern jets. To reach the museum, follow Pritchard Road northwards as it becomes Little River Road, also known as 'Military Row,' until you see the base on the right. Outside the museum there are three historic planes: a CF101 Voodoo, a CF100 Canuck all-weather interceptor and an Argus.

In 1876, a wharf was constructed at Comox and a Navy Training Base was established. The present base first opened in 1943 and operated for three years. With the end of World War II, it was not needed anymore and it closed. However, it reopened in 1952 and has been an active military base ever since.

*Note:* the ferry to Powell River (described in *Backroads of Southwestern British Columbia*) leaves from farther up the road, beyond the base, at Little River.

## FORBIDDEN PLATEAU & HEADQUARTERS

Return to where Comox Road meets the Island Highway and turn right. When you reach the junction with the old Island Highway, go straight through the traffic lights to turn off the Island Highway and continue on Headquarters Road.

If you are interested in going to Forbidden Plateau—which is well known for skiing, hiking, mountaineering and fishing—turn left onto Dove Creek Road shortly after you pass the Comox Valley Exhibition Grounds. After you cross the Tsolum River and the road curves to the right, turn left onto Piercy Road. Stay on Piercy Road until you reach its end at Duncan Bay Main and then continue on Forbidden Plateau Road—a total of 15.2 kilometres (9.4 miles)—to the parking lot for the ski lodge and chair lifts.

For the benefit of visitors, one of the lifts operates during the summer. From the point 1000 metres (3280 feet) above sea level where the lift ends, you can climb even higher, sit down and enjoy the great view of the Strait of Georgia and the Comox Valley. If you like, you can return to the lodge the whole way on foot.

In the winter, many skiers come from the southern part of the island and from the mainland to ski on the slopes of Forbidden Plateau and nearby Mount Washington. Both ski areas are outside Strathcona Provincial Park, which is a popular backcountry destination.

To get to Mount Washington, go back to where Forbidden Plateau Road meets Duncan Bay Main and turn left (north)—there is a sign. Turn left off Duncan Bay Main to follow Tsolum Main/Mount Washington Road, making sure to take the left

*Headquarters*

fork where the two diverge. It is about 25 kilometres (15.5 miles) from where you turned onto Duncan Bay Main to the Mount Washington Resort and Village.

Mount Washington, the operators of the resort boast, gets the highest annual snowfall of all the ski areas in British Columbia. In the summer, this mountain is also popular with mountain-bikers, hikers and horseback riders.

Return to Headquarters Road and turn left onto it. The road winds through farmland and out into the countryside. In 9.5 kilometres (5.9 miles) you come to a T intersection and a stop sign. Continue to the left, still on Headquarters Road. At kilometre 1.8 (mile 1.1), you reach a three-way stop sign. Go left onto Fitzgerald Road. In 0.5 kilometre (0.3 mile) is Farnham Road. Turn right onto it and at kilometre 0.8 (mile 0.5), before you cross the bridge, park in the pull-out to the right. Then follow the trail that goes into the tall trees.

**Forbidden Plateau** *The area was given the name Hiyu Cultus Illahe, meaning 'Plenty Bad Place,' by the Comox Natives. According to their legend of how the area got its name, the Comox Natives were being threatened by the Cowichan Natives, so the Comox men sent their families up onto the plateau. They believed that the land there was full of game to hunt, as well as being a safe place.*

*After the battle with their enemies, the men went looking for the women and children. They searched the forests and lakeshores of the plateau but could not find any trace of them. Believing that hairy giants had thrown everyone over the cliffs of what is now known as Cruickshank Canyon, they declared going to the plateau to be taboo. The taboo lasted for years and it is not certain if any local Natives have gone there since.*

You just get into the trees and on your right there is a huge concrete building, the only remains of the town of Headquarters. It is now used by partiers as a place to display their graffiti.

## MERVILLE, BLACK CREEK & MIRACLE BEACH

While you could return to Courtenay via Headquarters Road and head north from there, it is a shorter route to Highway 19 if you backtrack only as far as the T intersection where you turned left on you way to Headquarters. Continue straight ahead on Merville Road for 2 kilometres (1.2 miles) to Merville and Highway 19.

After the First World War, the Provincial Land Settlement Board chose the Merville area as a place for men returning from the battles in Europe to settle.

The next settlement, Black Creek, is stretched out along the highway. Farther down the highway, on the left at the turn-off for Miracle Beach Provincial Park, is 'Country Junction,' a market, deli and garden centre with ice cream, frozen yogurt, plants and vegetables for sale. There is even a play area to keep your children occupied while you shop.

Miracle Beach offers camping and is located next to where Black Creek empties into the ocean. Check at the mouth of Black Creek for hair seals and porpoises. Remember to just watch them—do not feed, chase or harass them—and keep your pets well away from them too.

**Headquarters**

*Headquarters was established at the northern end of the Comox Valley as the townsite for the Comox Logging and Railway Company. The company owned land in the area and cut hemlock trees. The logs were sent by train to Royston. From there they were floated across the strait to sawmills on the mainland. Hemlock, however, becomes waterlogged rapidly and the company was losing many of its logs. In 1914 the owners decided to build a sawmill on site. Equipment was brought over from England and the structure was made of concrete so that it would last. But it never sawed a log. There are two explanations. The first is that by the time the mill was ready to begin cutting, the First World War had broken out. Like other mills, it ceased operations because many of the men joined the forces. The second is that after the mill was completed, the company found out that it would be cheaper to send the logs to mills on the Fraser River.*

*The mill was dismantled, leaving the concrete hulk.*

After you cross the Oyster River, which has good fishing for trout, but before you reach the settlement of the same name, look to the left for the turn-off for the 600-hectare (1500-acre) University of British Columbia Research Farm. Students here study the breeding and feeding of a 350-head herd of dairy cattle, one of Vancouver Island's largest dairy herds. It is best to wear rubber boots or shoes that can be cleaned easily for your tour of the farm.

## OYSTER BAY & SHELTER BAY

You soon reach Oyster Bay, where there is a rest area on the shore. The beach is rocky, but you have a nice view of the ocean and the northern end of the Strait of Georgia.

You have occasional glimpses of the ocean as you drive towards Shelter Bay. Past Shelter Bay there is another rest area. It provides good views across Discovery Passage to the hills of Cape Mudge on Quadra Island. The passage got its name from Captain George Vancouver's sloop, the *Discovery*, which he sailed through here on July 13, 1792. His circumnavigation of the island that now bears his name proved that it was not part of the mainland, though it was Captain George Henry Richards, who surveyed these waters in 1865, who gets the credit for recognizing Georgia Strait to be a strait and not a gulf. The 60-metre (200-foot) high bluffs that you see were named after Lieutenant Zachary Mudge, who climbed them to take navigational observations for Captain Vancouver.

Since Discovery Passage is narrow and has rip tides, in 1898 a lighthouse was built to guide ships into the passage. During the day you can see the bluffs; in the evening you can see the light of the lighthouse flashing in the darkness.

Along this stretch of road, watch the treetops for bald eagles. Incidentally, the word 'bald' does not mean that it has no feathers. It comes from the word 'piebald,' because this eagle has two colours: dark brown with a white tail and a white head. However, an immature bird will have a brown head until it is about two years old.

From Shelter Bay, you can continue northwards for 2 kilometres (1.2 miles) to Campbell River and go on to see more of the northern part of Vancouver Island, and also take side trips to Quadra and Cortes islands (see Chapter 8).

*Steam Engine, Cortes*

to Woss and
Highway 19

*STRATHCONA
PROVINCIAL
PARK*

*Vernon
Lake*

Tahsis

*Nimpkish*

*Muchalat
Lake*

Rd

28

*Upana
Caves*

*Upana
Lake*

*Tahsis*

*Head
Bay*

*Moutcha
Bay*

Head Bay FS Rd

*River*

*Inlet*

Gold
River

*BLIGH
ISLAND
PROV.
MARINE
PARK*

mill

*Gold*

Yuquot

*Muchalat*

*Inlet*

*Nootka
Sound*

*Resolution
Cove*

# CAMPBELL RIVER to TAHSIS

*This trip, like several others in this book, is one where you will begin on the east coast of the island and end up on the west coast. After a tour of Campbell River, it will take you to Strathcona Provincial Park—Vancouver Island's largest park and the province of BC's oldest park—and on to the town of Gold River. Then you can take a (passenger-only) ferry to Nootka Sound and to the community of Tahsis—or, if you prefer, you can drive to Tahsis on a gravel logging road.*

*This route will give you opportunities to visit some of the Discovery Islands, fish from a salt-water pier and do some caving.*

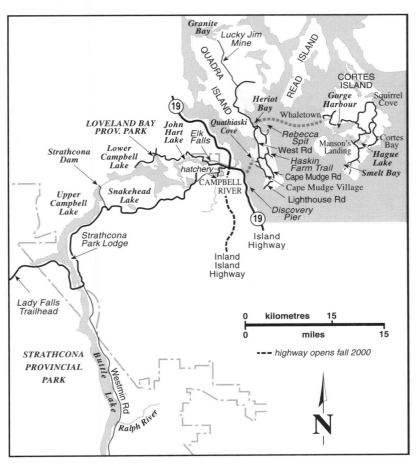

## CAMPBELL RIVER & AREA

As there is along much of the rest of Highway 19, there is beach to your right as you drive towards Campbell River from Shelter Bay. Watch for a huge, spray-painted rock, about 9 metres (30 feet) high, in the sand. It is easily seen from the highway. Most people know it as 'the Big Rock,' and geologists say that it was left here by the glaciers at the end of the last ice age.

According to Native legend, however, the Big Rock had a different origin: There was once a grizzly bear who claimed that he could leap from the mainland to Vancouver Island. He was warned by the Great Chief that if he touched water, he would turn to stone. Undeterred by the warning of the chief, the grizzly shot into the air. He almost made it, but when he landed on the beach, the tide had come in and so his back feet landed in the water. Thus, as the Great Chief had cautioned, he was turned into the rock that you see before you.

*Torii gates*

In case you want to stop and enjoy the beach or go for a stroll on the asphalt footpath along the shore, there is parking alongside the highway. At dusk, the ocean, with numerous boats anchored on its calm waters, is a beautiful sight. If you happen to drive by on a summer evening, watch for the flickering lights of beach fires out on the sand and the outlines of people as they walk around them.

You cross the 50th parallel, marked by a sign, as you drive through Campbell River and 1.7 kilometres (1.1 miles) beyond it, look for the large, orange Torii Gate, set on a grassed area above the ocean, on the right. There is no place to park in front of it, so pull onto a side street to park and walk back.

In Japan, where the native religion is Shintoism, Torii gates are built at the entrances to Shinto shrines. The first authentic Torii in Canada, this one was sent to Campbell River by its sister city of Ishikari, Japan, to celebrate the ongoing relationship between the two cities. Similarly, there is a totem pole carved by a local artist standing in Ishikari, sent by Campbell River to honour the peace and goodwill between the sister cities and our two nations.

The city of Campbell River, well known for its large trees and record Chinook salmon, started with just five settlers in 1900. With the beginning of lumbering and commercial fishing, however, settlement increased. The first hotel was built in 1904 and other buildings followed. Hydroelectric power came in the 1940s and a pulp and paper mill was built in the 1950s. Although Campbell River is geographically at about the halfway point on the island, it is generally thought of as part of the northern region—for many years it was the last stop on the road. It is now the major distribution point for the northern part of the island.

There are five different Pacific salmon in the area: the chinook, pink, chum, sockeye and coho. The chinook, the largest of the salmon family, can weigh as much as 32 kilograms (71 pounds). When they weigh over 13.6 kilograms (30 pounds), anglers call them 'Tyee,' from a Native word that means 'chief.'

The name 'Tyee' was first used for a fish caught in 1895 by Sir Richard Musgrave. The next year he published an article in *The Field*, an English journal. The article prompted British anglers to head to the Campbell River area to try their luck. In 1925, the Tyee Club of Campbell River was formed. Its unofficial headquarters was the Painter's Lodge. Inside it had hundreds of pictures of people from all walks of life with the Tyee that they had caught. The original building—along with all its mementos—burned down in 1985. A new one was constructed in 1987.

The Painter's Lodge Pub has what is believed to be the world's first and only salmon-skin bar. When a Tyee catch is recorded by an official, a bell is rung in the pub, signalling a round of drinks on the house.

The Tyee Club offers membership to any angler who catches a Tyee using club-regulation tackle and members now live all over the world. The record Tyee, which weighed in at 32 kilograms (71 pounds), was caught in 1968.

*Discovery Pier, Campbell River*

Discovery Passage, which continues northwards until it meets Johnston Straight and Nodales Channel near Rock Bay, narrows to about 2 kilometres (1.2 miles) between Vancouver Island and Quadra Island. This narrowing causes some of the strongest tides along BC's coast. All this tidal activity creates lots of food for the small fish that salmon feed on. Attracted by their prey, migrating salmon congregate by the thousands in the narrow passage just out from Campbell River.

*Discovery Pier, Campbell River*

If you want to try fishing for salmon but did not come equipped, just follow the highway to the Campbell River Salt Water Fishing Pier (the Discovery Fishing Pier) at the marina, to the right just as you enter downtown and near the ferry terminal. (Though you could not qualify as a Tyee Club member because of the rule about fishing from a rowboat.) Here you can get a daily fishing license and rent rods at the concession. There are even rod-holders attached along the sides of the 180-metre (590-foot) long wooden pier, and signs showing you what the different kinds of fish look like, to help you identify what you have caught. Then you can clean your fish at the fish-cleaning station so that you do not need to worry about what to do with the entrails—just enjoy your catch for supper. The pier is accessible to anglers in wheelchairs and has lowered sections of railings for their use.

This popular pier, opened in 1987, is usually full of anglers. If you think that you will not have much success fishing for salmon from a pier, just remember that the first year it was opened, a 22.2 kilogram (49 pound) Tyee was caught. Also, in that first year alone, there were 67 thousand visitors to the pier. While some came to watch—which is free—most came to fish.

If the pier is too crowded for you, you can charter a boat to go out into the passage and fish.

Continue along the highway past the pier and turn right at the terminal to take the ferry to Quadra Island (where you can go on to Cortes Island, if you wish).

## QUADRA ISLAND

As you come over on the 10-minute ferry ride from Campbell River, look to the right to see the village of Cape Mudge. In 1792, when Captain George Vancouver visited the North Coast Salish at what he named Cape Mudge, he found 350 people living in twelve wooden longhouses. During the early 1800s, the Lekwiltok Band of the Kwakwa'ka'wakw (sometimes written as 'Kwagiulth' or 'Kwakiutl') invaded the North Coast Salish and took over the cape. The We Wai Kai Band, descendants of the Lekwiltok, continue to live at Cape Mudge today.

All services are located on the southern part of the island, some within a short distance of your arrival point at Quathiaski Cove and more at Heriot Bay, near the ferry to Cortes Island. There are two campgrounds and a number of resorts and bed-and-breakfasts if you would like to overnight here.

Quadra Island is 34 kilometres (21 miles) long and roughly 9 kilometres (5.6 miles) wide. It does not belong to the Islands Trust, which looks after the Southern Gulf Islands and only the southern end of the island extends into the Strait of Georgia, so there is some dispute as to whether it too is a Gulf Island. Usually it is classified as the largest island of the Discovery Group (named after Captain Vancouver's ship, the *Discovery*.)

Besides the usual farming, logging, fishing and canning that the European settlers of Quadra worked at, some found employment in a successful gold mine, the Lucky Jim Mine. Opened in 1903, it is reported to have yielded hundreds of kilograms of gold and copper ore. The buildings and equipment were destroyed in a fire in 1925, after the mine was worked out and abandoned.

> **Whisky Point** *Whisky Point (which you can reach by going to the end of Noble Road) received its name during the Depression, when unemployed people built shacks along the south coast from Poverty Point, now known as April Point, around to Dogfish Bay. Whisky Point had a large number of residents who hand-trolled for salmon in dugouts, old rowboats and skiffs.*
>
> *When there was a good catch, some fishermen would go over to Campbell River to buy whisky for everyone to drown their problems and forget about their blisters. They also spent time 'shooting the bull' and the point was locally known as 'B.S. Point.'*

When you get off the ferry, begin by turning right onto Green Road to head for Cape Mudge, which you saw from the ferry. It is a nice, cool drive through the tall trees and you can see the waters of Discovery Passage to your right.

You can see the village of Cape Mudge as you near it. Watch for a little sign that directs you to the museum. Turn right down that road and you soon come to the Quadra Island United Church, the island's first Native church, consecrated in 1932.

The Kwagiulth Museum and Cultural Centre is past the church. Here you can peruse a collection of potlatch artifacts. The potlatch ceremony was banned by the federal government in 1884 but the Natives continued to hold them in secret.

*Cape Mudge church*

**Potlatches**  *Potlatch means 'to give' in the Chinook language. And give is what the person who put on the potlatch did. He gave away whatever material items he had. This giving spread the wealth of one man or family to the rest of the band. Those in need received— and when they had an abundance of goods, they in turn held a potlatch to reciprocate.*

*A potlatch might also be held by a person trying to save face or to apologize for bad behavior. Occasionally, hosts would try to outdo each other in the value of their gifts.*

*The non-Natives could not understand the concept of giving away material goods and they outlawed the celebrations from 1884 to 1951.*

*Today, a potlatch is held to mark an important event, such as a wedding, birth, naming or death.*

The ban was lifted in 1951 and the government agreed to give back the artifacts taken from three villages—Cape Mudge, Alert Bay and Village Island—if a museum was built to house them. The Kwagiulth Museum and Cultural Centre was built at Cape Mudge Village in 1979 and a similar facility was erected at Alert Bay (see Chapter 9). The museum at Cape Mudge is open from 10 AM to 4:30 PM daily, except Sunday, year-round.

Because of abuse and vandals, a number of rocks with petroglyphs on them were moved from various beaches around Quadra Island to the museum yard. Some are in the grass along the sidewalk leading to the building. Please look at them but if you want to make a petroglyph rubbing, there are casts especially made for the purpose located inside the museum.

To make a rubbing, spread a large piece of paper over the stone and rub a piece of boot wax (artists' charcoal or crayons will also work) across the paper, being careful not to tear it, until the impression comes through.

Go back to Green Road, turn right and drive southwards to Lighthouse Road. Turn left onto Lighthouse Road and go to Cape Mudge Road. Turn left again and go northwards to where you join Heriot Bay Road. Stay on Heriot Bay Road as it then curves to the right.

On the corner of Heriot Bay Road and Smith Road there is a sign that indicates the starting point for 'the Haskin Farm Trail to the Beach,' which is about one and one-half hours' walk return. Other trails cross this one all the way down to the beach, but just keep going straight. Watch out for bicyclists and horseback riders, who also use these trails. When you reach the beach, you have a great view of Cortes and Marina islands and the mountains on the mainland.

Continue on Heriot Bay Road and turn right onto Rebecca Spit Road. At the Rebecca Spit campsite there is a plaque that tells how this property was owned by Mr. and Mrs. Clandenning, who held many picnics here. In later years, the family let the community use it for their gatherings. As a result of those get-togethers, the land was eventually dedicated as a park for everyone to use.

It is about one hour's hike out to the tip of Rebecca Spit. As you walk, Drew Harbour is on your left and Sutil Channel is on your right. The spit used to belong to the We Wai Kai Natives but during the First World War the federal government traded some land nearby for it. The spit was then used for military purposes. The land was privately owned by another couple after the war and the province bought it and made it into a park in 1959.

Until 1946, the spit was one-third again as big as it is now. In that year an earthquake reduced its size by 1.2 hectares (3 acres) to what it is now—it became both shorter and narrower when the land dropped.

Return to Heriot Bay Road and continue until you reach a T intersection, where you can turn right to catch the ferry to Cortes Island.

To explore more of Quadra Island, turn left and then go right onto Hyacinthe Bay Road where it meets West Road. Eventually you reach Granite Bay Road on the left. This road goes past the site of the Lucky Jim Mine and on to Granite Bay. From 1900 to 1916, five hundred men were employed by a timber company at

*Petroglyphs, Quadra Island*

Granite Bay. A town was established here for them and their families—it had a school, a hotel, a store, a post office and a floating brothel. Today the northern part of the island is sparsely populated and few residents remain at Granite Bay.

## The Pirates of the West Coast

*Tales of piracy in Canadian waters have been largely confined to the East Coast and the Atlantic Ocean. The first recorded pirate there was Peter Easton, who raided French, English and Portuguese fishing fleets in harbours along Newfoundland's coast. Then there is the story of William Kidd, who is supposed to have buried treasure on Oak Island, off Nova Scotia's southern shore—it has still not been found, in spite of all the searching and digging. Yet one more notorious pirate of the many is Bartholomew Roberts, who, in June of 1720, attacked and captured twenty-two merchant ships at Trepassey, Newfoundland, and then hurried off to the Grand Banks, where he captured an additional six French vessels.*

*Few people, however, have heard of the West Coast piracy practised by a group of Euclataw Natives. From their hideout on Cape Mudge, a man on a hill would watch for a small group of Native or non-Native fur traders paddling their laden canoes through Discovery Channel on their way to Victoria. When he spotted a likely target, the lookout would summon the others and they would rush to their canoes and paddle feverishly up to the traders. Once alongside, they would rob them of their furs and other items of value and then take off again.*

*This area became known as 'the Hole of Death' because of the heavy winds, strong tides, whirlpools and the Euclataw pirates. Finally, a colonial gunboat was sent to patrol the waters, putting an end to the raids of these West Coast pirates.*

## CORTES ISLAND

You can get to Cortes Island by taking a 45-minute ferry ride from Heriot Bay on Quadra Island. Note that there are only five or six sailings per day in each direction and that the service shuts down by early evening. (When it is time to depart, it is best to leave before the second-to-last sailing of the day in order to avoid peak traffic.) As you ride between the two islands, watch for deer swimming from one island to the other.

The island is 25 kilometres (15.5 miles) long and 13 kilometres (8 miles) wide. The Spanish explorers named it for Hernando Cortes, who conquered Montezuma and the Aztecs of Mexico in the early 1500s. It was the Coast Salish who were the original Natives on this land, but many of them died in a smallpox epidemic in 1862. In the 1890s a different band, the Klahoose, came to the island from the north and their descendants still live at Squirrel Cove.

The ferry docks at Whaletown. While Natives had been hunting whales in the area already, the town got its name from a whaling station set up here by non-Natives in 1869. They slaughtered many whales for their oil before the station closed after only two years because of a decrease in the whale population.

There are general stores at Whaletown, Manson's Landing, Gorge Harbour, Squirrel Cove and Cortes Bay. If you wish to collect shellfish to eat for your lunch, there are a number of places to go: Manson's Landing Provincial Park has the easiest access to the beach. You can also try Squirrel Cove, Smelt Bay and south of the government wharf at Gorge Harbour. Check the limits and do not take more shellfish than you can eat. Stay away from the oyster and clam leases.

To reach Manson's Landing Provincial Park, take Whaletown Road from the ferry and then go right to continue on Gorge Harbour Road. When you get to Seaford Road, turn right and follow the signs to where you turn right into the park. The park consists of the strip of land between Hague Lake and Manson's Lagoon and also the marine spit at the entrance to the lagoon. If you want to lie on the sand or swim, go to the beach on Hague Lake. Since the lake provides the drinking water for the residents around it, you are asked not to use soap or shampoo in the water. Also to keep the water clean, camping and pets are not allowed on the beach and no power boats are allowed on the lake.

On the spit there are picnic tables where you can eat your lunch of shellfish or whatever else you have brought. You can walk along the spit, which was a midden of the Coast Salish who occupied this area for centuries. If the tide is low, you can explore southwards along the lagoon.

To reach Smelt Bay, where you can camp, get back onto Seaford Road and continue the short distance to Sutil Point Road. Turn right onto it and follow it southwards and westwards to Smelt Bay Road, where you turn right. The beach here is great for walking, collecting driftwood, picnicking and swimming.

If you want to explore more of the island, you can get a map at any of the general stores.

## ELK FALLS & STRATHCONA PROVINCIAL PARK

As you drive westwards on Highway 19 after passing through downtown Campbell River, when you get to where it turns right to cross over the Campbell River (and the Inland Island Highway comes from the left), continue straight on Highway 28, the Gold River Highway, instead.

If you would like to visit the Quinsam River Fish Hatchery, turn left onto Quinsam Road and follow it past Argonaut Road to the hatchery. Then continue along Highway 28 and less than 1 kilometre (0.5 half mile) from Quinsam Road there is a little pullout on the right where you can park and cross the Quinsam River on a pedestrian bridge. Take your rod and tackle and

*Elk Falls*

try fishing from the bridge. The Quinsam River is one of the best rivers on the island to fish for steelhead between December and March.

You have barely gotten back onto the highway when you reach the turn-off into Elk Falls Provincial Park campground. To see Elk Falls on the Campbell River, simply continue along Highway 28 to where it curves to the left at about kilometre 4.4 (mile 2.7) from the junction with Highway 19. At this point go straight ahead on the road to Elk Falls Provincial Park Picnic Area and Loveland Bay.

As you cross the one-lane wooden bridge, look to your left to see the John Hart Dam, one of several along this route built to generate electricity. Just after the bridge you reach a T intersection. Turn left if you want to go to Loveland Bay Provincial Park on Campbell Lake—a 17-kilometre (10.5-mile) drive. Otherwise, turn right to go into the Elk Falls Picnic Area and then take the second road to the right and follow it down into the parking lot for the Elk Falls Trail.

Follow the signs to the falls viewpoint. From the viewpoint you cannot see the waterfall very well because you are looking at it from the side. Though you can see where the water comes to the top and you can see it again part-way down, you do not see it actually plunging over the edge because of a short rock wall between it and you. Nevertheless, the gorgeous views of the deep canyon and high rock walls are well worth the visit.

## The Campbell River Fire of 1938

On July 5, 1938, a fire broke out in this area. Fifteen hundred loggers, area residents and unemployed men brought in from Vancouver fought the blaze for weeks as it swept through about 30,000 hectares (75,000 acres) of wooded and logged land.

The smoke was so heavy and dense throughout the region that the residents of Courtenay had to keep their lights on during the day. The wind blew the smoke as far southward as Portland, Oregon, and soot from the fire fell on the city of Vancouver.

Through their efforts, the firefighters' finally managed to stop the progress of the fire within 2.4 kilometres (1.5 miles) of the town of Campbell River. It was finally brought under control on August 1.

After the fire, the second largest on record in North America, the area was reforested and today it is hard for the untrained observer to see where any of the damage was done.

Back at Highway 28, turn right to continue to Strathcona Provincial Park. Watch for black bear along this winding road. At about kilometre 17.5 (mile 11) from Elk Falls Provincial Park, you reach a pull-out on the right with a beautiful view of the valley and Snakehead Lake below.

If you wish to have a picnic at the Strathcona Dam Recreation Site, watch for the turn-off to the right at 5.3 kilometres (3.3 miles) from the viewpoint. Turn right onto Strathcona Dam Road and drive to the earthfill dam. Situated at the bottom end of Upper Campbell Lake, the dam is 550 metres (1800 feet) wide and 52 metres (170 feet) tall.

Back on Highway 28, it is only a short distance past the road that leads to the dam before you are driving with Campbell Lake on your right. There are pull-outs from which you can take a look at the lake. As you drive farther, the road has more curves. You pass Strathcona Park Lodge 10.0 kilometres (6.2 miles) from when you first arrive at Upper Campbell Lake. Look for the statue of an elk 6.0 kilometres (3.7 miles) from the lodge, at Strathcona Provincial Park's Elk Portal.

One kilometre (0.6 mile) from the Elk Portal, keep right to stay on Highway 28 when you reach a junction from which Westmin Road heads southwards along the eastern shore of Buttle Lake, a lake popular with canoeists. If you went this way, you would pass the park headquarters, nature trails, picnic areas, swimming areas and boat launches. There is a campground at the mouth of the Ralph River and there are also a few designated tenting sites along some of the trails. At the end of the road is the Westmin Mine, for many years a source of concern for nature lovers who thought that that area should also be assigned full Class A park status.

If you do any camping in the park, either keep your food in your vehicle or hang it high in the air between a pair of trees to keep it from being eaten by the black bears that roam around at night. Do not keep food in or near your tent. Other wildlife that you might see include elk and wolverines.

As you continue towards Gold River from the junction, you immediately cross Buttle Narrows, which separates Buttle Lake from Upper Campbell Lake. If you look to your left you can see some small islands out in the narrows, one of which has a campground on it. In 2.0 kilometres (1.2 miles) from the junction, you reach the

Buttle Lake Campground. Buttle Lake was called Conuma Ahhook or 'Mountain Lake' by the Natives but was renamed after Commander John Buttle, one of the members of the first non-Native exploration party that discovered the lake in 1865.

After crossing Buttle Narrows, you work your way back northwards along the opposite shore of Upper Campbell Lake for a ways before following an arm of the lake to again head westwards. Along the way there are boat launches and recreation sites—you can camp, swim and fish.

After you leave the arm of the lake behind, you cross Filberg Creek. At 18 kilometres (11 miles) from the junction is the pull-out for Lady Falls Trail. It is a hike of less than 1 kilometre (0.5 mile) to a viewing platform. As you drive on, you continue to cross creeks and rivers. You leave the park just after Crest Creek Road and then the road begins a descent of 300 metres (1000 feet) past the town of Gold River to tidewater at Muchalat Inlet.

## GOLD RIVER

At kilometre 41.3 (mile 25.7) you reach the town of Gold River.

Gold River, a pulp mill town incorporated in 1965, was the first town in Canada with all-electric heating. Although Gold River has only about 2200 people and is a long way from the nearest large centre, it seems to lack none of the major amenities. For example, it has a library, five schools, a small college, a community centre, an indoor pool, a recycling program and the Village Plaza, with its numerous stores.

To reach tidewater, the pulp mill and the end of Highway 28, continue to the southwest, past the turn-off for Gold River Main, which goes northwest to join Highway 19 and has signs for the towns of Tahsis and Port Hardy. At 1 kilometre (0.6 mile) from the junction you cross the Gold River and follow it.

You pass the Gold River Lions Campground and then as you near the mill you can notice its characteristic smell. At kilometre 10 (mile 6) you come around a corner and you can see the white smoke billowing from the mill's stacks. At kilometre 12.6 (mile 7.8) you are at tidewater where the Gold River enters Muchalat Inlet.

### Strathcona Provincial Park

*Strathcona Provincial Park was named after Donald Alexander Smith, First Baron Strathcona and Mount Royal, who was a prominent person in the construction of the Canadian Pacific Railway. The park, formed in 1911, is the oldest in the province and comprises 232,350 hectares (574,130 acres) of mountain, forest, lakes, glaciers and rivers, of which 30,000 hectares (74,130 acres) were added in 1996.*

*The park's nickname of 'Little Switzerland' comes from its having six of the seven highest mountains on the island within its borders. The highest of them, and also the highest mountain in the Insular Range, is the Golden Hinde, whose peak reaches 2200 metres (7218 feet). The Comox Glacier, Vancouver Island's last glacier, is also in the park.*

*Della Falls, in the southern part of the park, is the second highest waterfall in Canada. The water plunges 440 metres (1443 feet) in three cascades. A 16-kilometre (10-mile) trail to the falls begins at the northwestern end of Great Central Lake (see Chapter 6), and there are also more rugged routes from elsewhere in the park.*

Pulp mill, Gold River

There are often line-ups of vehicles and boat trailers belonging to people who are out in the boats on the water.

The *MV Uchuck III*, a Second World War minesweeper that has been converted to haul passengers and supplies, leaves this dock for different destinations on different days of the week. On all of these cruises you will stop at settlements along the way to drop off supplies. As you go, watch for animals such as whales and sea otters in the water, bears along the shore and birds everywhere.

Every Tuesday, year-round, the *Uchuck III* heads out Muchalat Inlet and up Tahsis Inlet to Tahsis, stopping at logging camps and settlements along the way.

If you want to see Nootka Sound, the *Uchuck III* makes a trip there every Wednesday from the beginning of July to mid-September. On the way, the ship visits Resolution Cove, where Captain Cook first landed on the West Coast. Then it carries on to the settlement of Yuquot, also known as Friendly Cove.

In 1923, Yuquot became a National Historic Site. If you decide to get off the ship to explore Yuquot, you will be charged a landing fee, which goes towards the upkeep of this historic site by the Mowachaht/ Muchalaht Native Band, who are Nuu-chah-nulth (formerly Nootka). A guide will take you to an old Spanish fort, a historic church and a cemetery.

Dock, Gold River

Finally, the *Uchuck III* makes a two-day cruise to Kyuquot Sound every Thursday year-round. Its destination is Kyuquot, a Native settlement on Walter's Island. If you want to explore Kyuquot Sound up close, contact Slam Bang Lodge (phone 250-332-5313) and ask about renting a kayak to paddle your way along the shore and around the islands.

The waters between Nootka and Kyuquot sounds took 240 ships to their demise between 1803 and the 1950s. While modern technology has greatly improved maritime safety, a plane ride to view these waters, is also available if you would rather-take that option.

## TAHSIS

Before you leave Gold River, stock up on gas and groceries because there are no communities between here and Tahsis. Also, if you are interested in caving, stop in at the tourist information office for a map of the Upana Caves, which are on the way to Tahsis. Note that to visit the caves you should have a hard hat and a flashlight, which you can rent at the hardware store in Gold River. No matter what the tem-

**The First Europeans** *The first European to set foot on Vancouver Island was Captain James Cook of the HMS Resolution. He and his crew, along with the crew of the British Navy brig Discovery, had left the Sandwich (Hawaiian) Islands and headed towards the west coast of North America in search of the reputed Northwest Passage. (This Discovery was a different ship than the sloop of the same name that brought Captain Vancouver to the area some fourteen years later.)*

*After weeks in a storm off the Oregon coast, Cook and his crew headed northwards. They needed fresh water and wood to repair their vessels. They found shelter in an inlet that Cook first named 'King George's Sound' and then later renamed 'Nootka Sound.' It was early spring in the year 1778.*

*The Natives, whom Cook understood to be called 'Nootka' (the Nuu-chah-nulth) came out in their huge canoes to see the ships. They did not come aboard but the next day they came back with goods to trade. On the following day the ships were moved to what the seafarers dubbed 'Ship Cove,' now called Resolution Cove. The cove (today part of a provincial marine park) is on Bligh Island, which was named after the master of the Resolution, William Bligh. (Bligh went on to become the master of the Bounty, and is perhaps best known for the 1789 mutiny in which he and eighteen other crewmen were set adrift.)*

*The repairs took longer than first thought and during that time the Europeans and the Natives held a brisk trade. The Natives, under their leader, Chief Maquinna, offered sea otter furs, fish and oil in trade for knives, nails and anything made of metal. They were especially fond of brass.*

*On April 20, Cook and some of his crew paddled around the sound, stopping at Yuquot, where they found a Native village. He named the place 'Friendly Cove' because of the warm welcome that they received. It was noon on April 26, 1778, when the two ships left Bligh Island.*

*A quarter-century later, in 1803, Chief Maquinna and a group of his men attacked the ship Boston after the captain of the ship embarrassed the chief by calling him a liar. John Jewitt—an ironworker—and a sailmaker named Thompson survived the attack and were kept as slaves for two years. They were rescued by the brig Lydia, and for the next one hundred years, ships avoided that coast, fearing attacks. The fur trade in this area died as a result.*

**Caving** Gold River has been the headquarters of the British Columbia Speleological Association since 1978, when it was founded. The town began calling itself 'the Caving Capital of Canada' in 1984.

There are more than one thousand known caves on Vancouver Island and most of them are on the northern part of the island. The longest is Thanksgiving Cave, with a mapped length of 7.6 km (4.7 miles). Over fifty of these caves are in the area between Gold River and Nootka Sound and some of them are several kilometres (miles) long. The Upana Caves are among the easiest to reach and are a good choice if you want to see a cave without going too far in or are a beginner at caving.

A cave is formed over many centuries, most often in limestone formations. Water, when combined with carbon dioxide, forms a solution of carbonic acid. Although the solution is weak, over the years the acid slowly dissolves some of the limestone and passageways are formed. When water carrying dissolved limestone slowly evaporates, the mineral is left behind, creating stalactites, stalagmites and other features.

In Canada, we use the word 'caving' to describe this underground experience. In the US, the term 'spelunking' is more common. It comes from the Latin word spelunca, which means 'cave.'

perature is outside, the caves generally stay at about 7 degrees Celsius (45 degrees Fahrenheit), so bring along a jacket. Also wear long pants and sturdy, rubber-soled boots.

As you head northwards from Gold River and Highway 28 on Gold River Main (the first part of which is also called the Tahsis Road) it begins as pavement but it is narrow and in bad shape. At kilometre 2.8 (mile 1.7), just after you cross the Gold River, you reach a stop sign. Turn left onto the Head Bay Forest Service Road to go to Tahsis. (If you wish to skip Tahsis and go straight to Woss and Port Hardy, turn right.)

You immediately cross a one-lane bridge over the Upana River and are on gravel. Then there is another one-lane bridge at kilometre 4.2 (mile 2.6). Just past that bridge, take the next main road to the right. Narrow and winding, this road begins to climb. Watch out for gravel trucks, logging trucks and falling rocks.

The logging roads that you are following from Gold River to Tahsis form the route for 'the Great Walk,' which takes place in early June each year.

Since participants have only one day to do this 63.5-kilometre (39.4-mile) walk, only the truly fit need consider planning to do the whole route. Start time is 4 AM. If you make it to the middle of the twelve checkpoints, you get a T-shirt; if you finish, you get a 'burning boot' trophy.

In the first twenty years following its start in 1977, the walk raised nearly one million dollars in the form of pledges to various charities. There is an entry fee and you must pre-register (phone 250-934-6570 for more information).

At kilometre 18.0 (mile 11.2) from the junction with Highway 28, you come to a turn-off on the right (marked by a sign) for the Upana Caves. Turn right and in just 0.2 kilometre (0.1 mile) you reach a wide, open space along the road where you can park, with a green toilet facility in the bush above the area. Then walk back

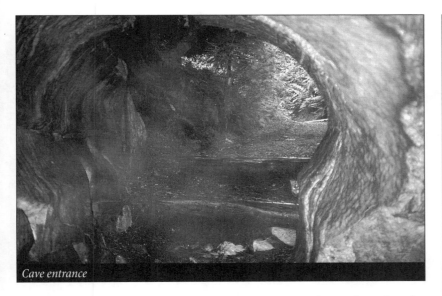

*Cave entrance*

down the road to where the trail to the caves begins. A sign facing the parking lot directs you to the caves.

When you turn off the road onto the path, you begin by walking through an old-growth forest of western hemlock, yellow-cedar and western white pine, some of which are over two hundred years old. After a short distance you enter a young forest.

Just follow the path and within minutes you reach the first cave. However, the opening is small and if you wish to enter it, you will need to crawl backwards to do so. You might change your mind when you discover that it is called 'Insect Cave,' because it is home to crickets and spiders. The opening to the second cave is not much bigger, so carry on to the third one. It has steps in the rock that you can walk down and you can really explore. Other caves are named 'Main Cave,' 'Tunnel Cave,' 'Corner Cave' and 'Resurgence Cave.'

In order to preserve the caves for the enjoyment of others, please ensure that no members of your party leave any litter, disturb the insects and other living creatures, touch the delicate formations, smoke or light fires.

A few minutes' drive after the caves you reach a Y in the road. Turn right to stay on Head Bay Forest Service Road and continue towards Tahsis. A little farther along you pass Moutcha Bay Resort, the only resort on the road. After Moutcha Bay comes Head Bay,

*Upana Caves*

Quadra Island from ferry

then Malaspina Lake and Perry Lake and then you reach Tahsis. It is slow going and could take a few hours of driving.

Tahsis is a pretty village with houses surrounded by tall trees overlooking the water. If you are looking for a small, quiet retreat with atmosphere and nice beaches, this is the place to go. There are two motels and two recreational vehicle parks, a small marina, a few stores, several restaurants, a museum and a school. It has retained a quiet peacefulness where you can really relax. The beaches are sandy, with huge, sun-bleached logs. For a change of pace, there are hiking trails, tours of the town and good fishing.

While Tahsis itself is close to the end of the road, as you head back towards the east coast of the island there are plenty of logging roads to explore if you so desire. Just remember that they are owned by the logging companies and you may need permission. Some are closed to public traffic during working hours on the weekdays. Always drive safely and with your headlights on.

You can take the same logging roads that you took to get here to go back to Gold River and then return along Highway 28 to Campbell River. From there you can head northwards to explore the most northerly part of Vancouver Island (see Chapter 9). As an alternative, once you hit Gold River Main, turn left and head to the northwest to take a shortcut to Highway 19 near Woss (see Chapter 9).

## First Non-Native Settlers

*In 1778, Captain John Meares brought workers from China to construct and look after his fur-trading base at Nootka. These workers also built the first schooner to be sailed on the west coast of Vancouver Island. It was called the North West America.*

*When the Nootka War broke out between the Spanish and the English, the Chinese labourers were taken prisoner by the Spanish. The Spanish put them to work looking after the Spanish post and working a small gold-field at the head of Muchalat Inlet. It is believed that some of the labourers married into the local Native tribe but their final fate is not known.*

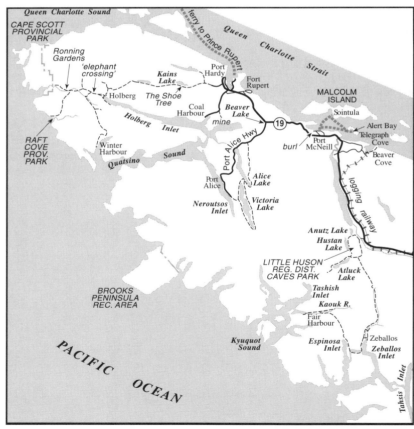

# CHAPTER 9

# SEYMOUR NARROWS to PORT HARDY

*If you have just come from exploring the area to the west of
Campbell River, after all those narrow roads with curves, hills and
drop-offs, this paved route to Port Hardy will be a pleasure to
drive. Highway 19 is mainly straight, mainly flat and nice and wide.
Your route cuts away from the ocean and, except for a stop in
Sayward on Johnstone Strait, it will not go near the ocean again
until you are almost at Port McNeill.*

*The most northerly part of Vancouver Island is largely
wilderness. Wildlife is abundant and the scenery is beautiful, but
the area is subject to strong winds and the heavy rainfall makes it
one of the wettest in Canada.*

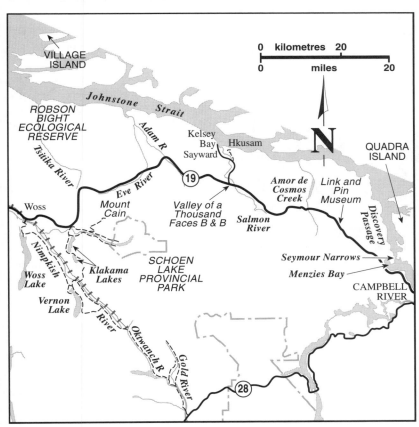

## SEYMOUR NARROWS

As you drive northwards from Campbell River on Highway 19, you are travelling beside Discovery Passage. Watch for the Ripple Rock Rest Area and Seymour Narrows Lookout on your right, 11.0 kilometres (6.8 miles) from the junction of Highways 19 and 28. The lookout has an elevation of 52 metres (170 feet).

Ever since Captain George Vancouver first sailed through Seymour Narrows in 1792, Ripple Rock, beneath the waters of the narrows, had been sinking unlucky ships that ventured into the narrows. The rock had two peaks, one less than 6 metres (20 feet) under water at low tide and the other less than 3 metres (10 feet) beneath the surface. These two hidden summits caused over 120 shipwrecks, 20 of which were major ones, and took 114 lives. Mariners sailing ships to Prince Rupert and Alaska found that the safest option was to wait for high tide before proceeding.

*Seymour Narrows, Ripple Rock*

Finally, in 1955, the government decided to do something about this submerged rock. Over the next two and one-half years, workers drilled a 175-metre (570-foot) shaft on nearby Maude Island and built a 'raise' (another tunnel going upwards) to reach under the two peaks. They drilled many 1.2 x 1.8-metre (4 x 6-foot) tunnels and plugged them with a total of 1250 thousand kilograms (2756 thousand pounds) of Nitramex 2H, a high-powered explosive— enough to fill thirty-four railway boxcars. Pessimists predicted that there would be tidal waves and collapsing buildings because of the explosion. As a precaution, the town of Campbell River turned off all public services.

At 9:31 AM on Easter Sunday, April 5, 1958, the button was pushed and one of the world's largest non-atomic explosions took place. An estimated 630 thousand tonnes (700 thousand tons) of rock and water were hurtled into the sky as television cameras watched and recorded. When everything had cleared, the top of Ripple Rock was 14 metres (47 feet) below the surface. No window had broken, no wharf had collapsed and no boat had been overturned by the blast. The total cost of setting off this explosion had been $3.1 million dollars.

From this viewpoint you can look out over the narrows. They do not appear any different than they did before the blast because the peaks were under water. But even though the peaks are gone, vessels still have to be careful of the swirling eddies, the dangerous currents and the rip tides. It is hard to believe that this beautiful spot could be so hazardous.

After the lookout, you catch glimpses of the narrows through the trees. Then you reach Menzies Bay, with an outcropping of land into the water, and after that you turn away from Discovery Passage.

If you want to hike down to the shore of Seymour Narrows, look for the Ripple Rock Hiking Trail 6.7 kilometres (4.2 miles) from the Seymour Narrows Lookout and turn right into the parking lot. However, the trail is rugged and not well-maintained and there is not a lot to see.

Then, at kilometre 20.6 (mile 12.8) from the lookout, you reach the Link and Pin Museum, which is named after the link-and-pin-style couplers that were once

## Captain George Vancouver

*At the age of sixteen, on a voyage to the Antarctic in 1773, George Vancouver served as a midshipman for Captain Cook, who was soon to become the first European to set foot in what is now BC (see 'The First Europeans' on p.141). Then, in 1791, Vancouver was captain of the HMS Discovery when it and the Chatham left England charged with searching the BC coast for the rumoured Northwest Passage. His orders also included charting the rest of the west coast of North America that Cook had not already charted.*

*Vancouver and his men spent time exploring the waters between Vancouver Island and the mainland before meeting the Spanish ships the Mexicana and the Sutil, commanded by Dionisio Alcala Galiano and Cayetano Valdes. They, too, had been charting the strait. Vancouver suggested that they continue together.*

*When one of his men announced that he had found a northwest passage to the Pacific Ocean, Vancouver and his two ships sailed on alone without the Spaniards. They anchored at Cape Mudge, on Quadra Island while Vancouver and some of his men went ashore to visit the Natives.*

*They continued on their quest, rounding the northern end of what is now Vancouver Island and then sailing southwards to Nootka where their supply ship was waiting. Although he had not found the Northwest Passage, Vancouver had proven that the mass of land that now bears his name was in fact an island, separate from the mainland. (Nevertheless, it fell to Captain Henry Richards, in 1865, to rename 'The Gulf of Georgia' as a strait.)*

*From 1778 onwards, traders from England, Russia, the United States and Spain had been active in the Nootka Sound area. Then, in 1789, the Spanish had captured two British ships and sent them to Mexico. The problem was supposedly rectified and another of Vancouver's tasks was to oversee the return of the trading territory to Britain.*

*Captain Vancouver and the Spanish governor of the area, Juan Francisco de la Bodega y Quadra, met at Friendly Cove. They could not arrive at a settlement. Vancouver sailed southwards in October and then westwards to the Sandwich (Hawaiian) Islands for the winter. He returned to continue his exploration of the northern mainland coast the next year. The dispute between the two countries was referred back to London and Madrid and eventually the Spanish left the island.*

*Link and Pin Museum*

used to lock railway cars together. The museum features displays of the logging and railway history of the area and has artifacts, such as kerosene lamps, to look at. Some of the highway in this area is part of the old logging railway bed that was used to haul the logs down to the water.

Along this part of the highway there are signs that tell when the trees in each area were first cut, when new ones were planted, when they were thinned and when the area will be cut again. If you wish to get some exercise, stop and try one of the hiking trails along the way.

One of the many creeks and rivers that you cross is Amor de Cosmos Creek, at kilometre 30.8 (mile 19.1). It was named after the second premier of the province, Amor de Cosmos ('Lover of the Universe'), whose term ran from 1872 to 1874. His real name was William Alexander Smith. He came to BC from Nova Scotia and started *The British Colonist* newspaper in Victoria in 1858.

Watch for Dalrymple Creek Nature Trail, an interpretive trail through the forest, at kilometre 45.7 (mile 28.4). Then, if you wish to buy some honey, stop at the honey farm at kilometre 49.1 (mile 30.5).

## SAYWARD

You have been following the Salmon River, on the left, for some distance when you cross it at kilometre 52.1 (mile 32.4), near where it turns to flow northwards past Sayward and Kelsey Bay to Johnstone Strait. Some of the island's largest steelheads have been taken from this river. Just 2 kilometres (1.2 miles) from the Salmon River crossing you take a turn to the right onto Cemetery Road to go to Sayward. But first take note of the Thousand Faces Bed-and-Breakfast across the highway from the turn-off.

*Cable House Restaurant*

As soon as you turn off the highway towards Sayward, you come to a traffic light that alternates vehicle flow over the arched, one-lane bridge across the Salmon River.

On the other side of the bridge, you pass the Cable House Restaurant to your left. This steel-framed building is appropriately named—about 2450 metres (8000 feet) of used logging cables went into its construction. The restaurant, which opened in 1970, weighs almost 24 tonnes (26 tons).

*Memorial cairn*

Continue towards the village of Sayward and at about kilometre 5 (mile 3) you come to a road called 'the Port Hkusam Trail' on the right just before you cross the long, wide concrete bridge over the Salmon River. Turn right onto this side road and then immediately make a left. Drive a short distance to the entrance for the Armishaw Lodge, established in 1913, and the Port Hkusam Trail (this part is for walking). On each side of the entrance there is a stone-and-concrete pillar. The one on the right has fallen over.

The story of the pillars is as follows: In 1913, John and Jane Armishaw and their family moved to Sayward from the mainland. John became the Justice of the Peace for the area. He also crusaded for the building of a road to Campbell River and Cape Scott. In 1943, the Armishaws celebrated their 50th wedding anniversary and the stone pillars were built to mark the land where their house once stood. Look at the bottom of the plaque on the right pillar to read these words:

*'Blessed be they that spare these stones, but cursed be they that remove them.'*

Back at Cemetery Road, turn right to arrive in Sayward, which is on the bay off Johnstone Strait into which the Salmon River flows. The village, which grew slowly, was named after William Sayward, who moved to Vancouver Island in 1858 and worked in the lumber business. And here is a tidbit from history: in 1902, when Mr. Otto Sacht built his store here, he used a single fir plank 9.8 metres (32 feet) long as his counter.

From Sayward (or from Telegraph Cove, which this route visits later) you can take a boat tour to Robson Bight Ecological Reserve, located about halfway between Sayward and Port McNeill, on the southwestern shore of the northwestern end of Johnstone Strait. The

## Valley of a Thousand Faces

*The previous owner of the property now owned by the Thousand Faces Bed-and-Breakfast was a painter named Hetty Fredrickson. She painted faces and animals on large, round slabs of wood and then hung them from tree limbs throughout her acreage. Visitors would wander along the paths where these painting hung. They enjoyed her work as well as the stroll through the trees. Eventually her acreage became known as the Valley of a Thousand Faces.*

*Before she died, she sold her paintings, giving friends who had favourites the first chance to buy them. The present owners have kept the name of the property and turned the house into a bed-and-breakfast. You can stop in and stroll through the paths as it is still an enjoyable visit, even though the faces are gone from the trees.*

*There are two faces left, and they are on the outside wall of the house. If you would like to see more of the paintings, many of them are at the Zeballos Hotel in Zeballos (which you will visit later in this chapter).*

reserve was set aside to protect a 'rubbing beach' where orcas (killer whales) rub themselves against the gravel in the shallow water at the edge of the strait, one of only a handful of such sites in the world.

If you continued 1 kilometre (0.6 mile) farther along the road beyond Sayward, you would arrive at the settlement of Kelsey Bay. Up until 1892, a Native village was located there at the mouth of the Salmon River.

As you continue westwards along Highway 19, you occasionally drive between canyon walls. At one point the road climbs for a ways and you are able to see a valley below. The purple lupines are beautiful here.

## THE NIMPKISH VALLEY & WOSS

You cross the Adam River at kilometre 29.7 (mile 18.5) from the Sayward junction. Then you go downhill and once in the valley you come to the Eve River at kilometre 39 (mile 24.2). Just beyond there is a rest area on the Eve River. Then, at kilometre 56.6 (mile 35.2), a welcome sign greets you as you enter the Nimpkish Valley.

If you want to visit Schoen Lake Provincial Park—where you can camp, picnic, swim, hike or fish—or the Mount Cain Ski Area—where you can hike in the summer—turn left onto the East Klaklakama logging road at kilometre 65.9 (mile 40.9) and then left again onto Davie Road. If you were to stay on the East Klaklakama logging road, it would take you southwards past the Klaklakama Lakes and meet up with the road from Woss to Gold River near Vernon Lake.

Take the turn-off for Woss, to the left at kilometre 79.8 (mile 49.6). You cross the Nimpkish River and come to a T intersection. To visit the combined settlement of Woss and Woss Camp—which has a few houses, a service station and a restaurant—go to the right.

Also at Woss is the headquarters for Canadian Forest Products Englewood Logging Division. The company runs a 122-kilometre (76-mile) private logging railway in the Nimpkish Valley, one of the longest railways of this type in North America. Logs from here are taken westwards and then northwards to Beaver Cove (next to Telegraph Cove), lashed together to form booms and towed 320 kilometres (200 miles) to a sawmill on the mainland.

If you would like to take one of the company's tourist rides along part of the logging railway to Beaver Cove, or if you are planning to travel along

### The Nimpkish Valley

*The Nimpkish Valley begins as far southward as Vernon Lake. It then follows a wavy line to the northwest—taking in Woss Lake, Atluck Lake and Anutz Lake—and then northwards along Nimpkish Lake and also takes in Port McNeill. It is full of lakes and rivers, hiking trails, picnic areas and attractions. If you enjoy exploring logging roads, the Nimpkish Valley has more than 480 kilometres (300 miles) of them.*

*In earlier times, Natives who had their summer home at the mouth of the Nimpkish River travelled through this valley via the Nimpkish River and Nimpkish Lake for the first part of their trip to Muchalat Inlet on the west coast of the island, where they overwintered. They switched over to the Oktwanch and Gold rivers for the rest of the way.*

the logging roads in the area and want a map, stop in and ask at the Canadian Forest Products office. (Note that this route passes Beaver Cove later on.)

If, instead of turning right to go into Woss, you took the left turn at the T intersection, you would be on a logging road, Rona Road, which goes southwards to Gold River. Until 1978, this road was the only one connecting the northern part of Vancouver Island with the rest. There are signs along the way to direct you on this 83-kilometre (52-mile) gravel road if you want to drive it.

A short distance down this road from your starting point at the T junction you would have the choice of heading for Woss Lake (where you could camp or fish) or turning left to continue onwards to Gold River. Further along on the way you would pass the Nimpkish Island Ecological Reserve on the Nimpkish River and then come to the turn-off for Vernon Lake (where you could also camp or fish). After Vernon Lake, now on Nimpkish Road, you would follow the Nimpkish River awhile longer and then follow the Oktwanch River on your right as it flows to Muchalat Lake. After the lake, you would continue southwards to follow the Gold River on Gold River Main until you arrived in the town of Gold River (see Chapter 8).

# Zeballos to Telegraph Cove

## THE LITTLE HUSON CAVES & ZEBALLOS

From the turn-off for Woss, continue along Highway 19 for 21.5 kilometres (13.4 miles) and then turn left onto the road to Zeballos. There is a large sign at the junction for Little Huson (formerly 'Hustan') Regional District Caves Park. Signs direct you to the park, so the distances given, which are from the highway junction, are just for reference.

At kilometre 1.4 (mile 0.9) you reach a Y where you go to the left. Just past the Y you cross a concrete bridge over the Nimpkish River, which is a long way below. Drive with your lights on as it is very dusty. When you reach the T intersection at kilometre 2.7 (mile 1.7), turn right, towards Zeballos.

At 3.1 kilometres (1.9 miles), you reach a Y, where left goes to Zeballos. Go right instead to visit the Little Huson Caves. At 5.8 kilometres (3.6 miles), you reach a junction. Turn left towards the caves and Atluck Lake. (Anutz Lake Road goes straight ahead.) At kilometre 7.1 (mile 4.4), go to your right and at the Y, just beyond, go left. This road gets narrower but is still driveable with any vehicle.

At kilometre 7.9 (mile 4.9) you reach a road to the right. According to the sign back at the highway, you should park here if you have a large vehicle, and then you continue on foot. There is a sign cautioning 'overhanging branches' but though the branches do meet overhead, a motorhome could make it. And though there is one place where the road has started to fall away, with care any vehicle could make it by. If you do decide to walk, it is only a 2.3-kilometre (1.4-mile) hike to the parking lot. The road is like a country lane with grass growing in the middle while the spreading branches of the tall trees create a dim and parklike setting beneath.

In 10.2 kilometres (6.3 miles) from the highway you reach the large parking lot at Little Huson Regional District Caves Park. The trail starts to the right and it is a 15-minute walk from the lot. Keep to the designated trails in this karst area, because of the danger of falling into a sinkhole or cave in the limestone hidden beneath the debris on the forest floor.

On your way to the caves, you reach a wooden platform from which you can look down into pools of water. From there, the trail leads to the two caves that are open to the public. They are larger than the Upana Caves north of Gold River (see Chapter 8), with wider entrances. You do not need a flashlight, because the daylight reaches in as far as you can go.

The park and caves are looked after by the Regional District of Mount Waddington (phone 250-956-3301). For information on tours of other caves in the area, contact Mountain Line Tours and Travel Ltd. (250-956-4827).

To continue on to Zeballos, one option is to return to where you left the road to Atluck Lake and follow it past Hustan Lake to a junction where it meets Atluck Road. Go left towards Zeballos—or go to the right a short ways if you want to stop at Atluck Lake first—and then turn right onto Pinder Main after 3.3 kilometres (2.1 miles).

Another way is to return all the way back to where you turned right at the Y 3.1 kilometres (1.9 miles) off the highway. This time take the other fork towards Zeballos. Then take the left fork onto Pinder Main when you reach the southern end of Mukwilla Lake.

Just past the junction at Mukwilla Lake, you pass Wolfe Lake on the right. You follow Pinder Creek for a ways and then cross the Zeballos River twice before arriving at the village of Zeballos and crossing it a third time.

The small village of Zeballos on Zeballos Inlet was big enough to have its own newspaper in the heyday of the gold mines. Much smaller today, its primary resource is timber. Most visitors who come here do so to see what life is like in a small village on the west coast of Vancouver Island. If you have a boat with you, there is a small dock from which to launch it to explore some of the west coast.

While in town, stop in at the Zeballos Hotel, originally the Pioneer Hotel when it was built in 1938. Look at the figures and faces on its walls—they came from the Valley of a Thousand Faces at Sayward, mentioned earlier in this chapter. The owners bought many of the pieces of art and put some up on the outside of their hotel, some in the yard and many others on display inside.

## FAIR HARBOUR

Another place to go to launch your boat for some exploration or to camp for the night is Fair Harbour, an hour's drive from Zeballos and easy to find because your way is marked with signs. You begin by recrossing the Zeballos River on the wooden bridge that you took on your way into town. Turn left at the stop sign to follow Fair Haven Main southwards along Zeballos Inlet for 5.1 kilometres (3.1 miles) until you reach a junction. If you wish to camp on Zeballos Inlet, go straight ahead a short ways to the campsite. Otherwise, turn right to stay on Fair Harbour Main.

As you drive, Little Espinosa Inlet is to your right for a ways and then the road turns northwards to take you along the northern part of Espinosa Inlet. The road continues northwards until it crosses the Kaouk River. It turns westwards and reaches Fair Harbour at the southern end of Tahsish Inlet, 33.3 kilometres (20.7 miles) from the stop sign in Zeballos. Fair Harbour was once the site of a logging camp but now you find only a campsite and a dock. If you have a canoe, kayak or other boat, you might want to explore the shoreline. Water taxis are available to take you to other logging camps or to the Native village of Kyuquot on Kyuquot Sound.

## BEAVER COVE & TELEGRAPH COVE

Back at Highway 19, turn left to continue northwards. In 8.4 kilometres (5.2 miles) you reach a turn-off to go down to the shore of Nimpkish Lake. Advanced windsurfers will want to try this lake, considered to be one of the best lakes in the province for the sport.

The highway then follows long, narrow Nimpkish Lake for many kilometres (miles) as it takes you through forest, across creeks and between rock walls.

Soon after you leave Nimpkish Lake, turn right onto Kilpala Road to go to Beaver Cove and Telegraph Cove. You cross Theimer

*Beaver Cove*

*Telegraph Cove*

Creek #2 and Theimer Creek #1 in the first kilometre (0.5 mile). At kilometre 19.6 (mile 12.2) from Highway 19 you come to a stop sign. Beaver Cove and Telegraph Cove are to the left on the gravel road.

Then you drive over a one-lane arched wooden bridge with limited visibility. To the right of this bridge there is a historic railway trestle, still in use, over the Kokish River, part of the logging railway mentioned in the section on the Nimpkish Valley and Woss. At the Y, go right and when you reach a stop sign at a set of railway tracks, do stop and check for trains because, as the sign reads, 'any time is train time.'

You reach Beaver Cove at kilometre 1.5 (mile 0.9) from the junction. There is a large log-sorting ground here, with lots of log booms out in the water. Pull to the left to park and watch the tugs moving those large logs and log booms around.

Afterwards, you can see Beaver Cove to your left as the road climbs. At the next stop sign, turn left to go to Telegraph Cove. You reach pavement and in less than 1 kilometre (0.6 mile) from the beginning of the pavement you get to Telegraph Cove.

Telegraph Cove is a very popular place, so it might be hard to find a parking spot. Tour buses, campers, boaters and sightseers—everyone stops at the cove. Many are here for the whale-watching tours and others come to see one of the last towns whose buildings and homes are on stilts or pilings

*Telegraph Cove*

**Orcas** *If you look out into the water and you see some black-and-white whales, you are watching orcas, formerly known as killer whales. The male can weigh over 8000 kilograms (17,600 pounds) while the female is slightly smaller, at up to 7000 kilograms (15,400 pounds). The newborn calf is about 2 metres (6.5 feet) long, while its mother would typically be about 6 metres (20 feet) and its father 8 metres (26 feet).*

*A pod (extended family group) may consist of between five and twenty cows, calves and bulls. Along the Pacific coast between Alaska and Washington State, there are an estimated 30 orca pods. During the summer, 19 of these pods visit Johnstone Strait.*

*Orcas go through a number of manoeuvres as they swim in the ocean. Researchers have identified and named different types of behaviours. For instance, a whale might hit the water with its flippers or tail, which is known as 'fluking.' Or it may lift the upper part of its body out of the water and look around, an activity called 'spyhopping.'*

*The whistles, moans and squeaks that they use to communicate can be heard for up to 11 kilometres (7 miles) and are different within each pod. Orcas also have a sonar system that helps them to locate their prey.*

*Orcas are toothed whales (as distinguished from baleen whales). While they may hold their prey—such as fish or squid—between their peglike teeth before swallowing, they do not chew their food. A male orca may eat up to 900 kilograms (2000 pounds) of food per day.*

above the water. Walk out onto the dock to see the historic buildings on their stilts, then wander down the boardwalk to see them up close.

The town of Telegraph Cove was built in the 1920s and 1930s and it received its name because it was at the northern end of a telegraph line that was strung from tree to tree along the east coast of the island. Until this last part of Highway 19 was constructed in 1979, a ferry ran up-island from Kelsey Bay to Beaver Cove.

The residents have tried to retain the early twentieth-century look of the area. The buildings all have write-ups on them explaining their uses over the years. Remember, though, that some of them are still privately owned so do not go tramping through them without checking first.

One of the buildings, the Nakamura House, was built by Japanese immigrants and then served as the office for fish-salting operations in Telegraph Cove. Another one, a long, red building, is the Air Force Mess Hall. It got its name during the Second World War when the Air Force commandeered the local sawmill. Military personnel then operated the machinery to cut lumber to help build bases farther up the island in Port Hardy and nearby Coal Harbour and also up the mainland coast in Bella Bella. After the war, the local mill used this building as its cookhouse. During the 1950s, this building doubled as the community hall.

If you want to do some whale-watching, you can book a tour to Robson Bight. If you canoe or kayak, you might want to try the 20-kilometre (12-mile) paddle along Johnstone Strait from the cove to the bight.

*Telegraph Cove*

Robson Bight is an ecological reserve formed in 1982 to protect the orca habitat. The whales come here to feed on the migrating salmon during the summer. They play offshore and swim up to the shore at Robson Bight to rub on the gravel near the mouth of Tsitka River.

Because this area has been set aside for the benefit of the whales, a number of regulations apply: Boats are not to get closer than 100 metres (330 feet) from the whales, nor are they to speed or make sudden changes in direction. Visitors should keep quiet, not venture onto the bight itself when the whales are rubbing and not camp there overnight.

There is a campsite here at Telegraph Cove if you wish to spend a couple of days seeing the area.

Just before you get back to Highway 19 as you retrace your route, turn into the North Island Forestry Information Centre. If your spouse is here for a week of fishing and you are tired of fishing, book one of the 'forest discovery tours.' There are five tours to choose from, taking in different north-island forested areas, each operated by a different timber company.

While you can book here, each tour begins at the tourist information booth in either Port McNeill or Port Hardy. Depending on the tour, you can do such things as stop and talk to the loggers or plant a tree. Expect to learn about various aspects of the forest industry, to see some clear-cutting and to tour both second-growth forest and old-growth forest.

Wear sturdy shoes because you will be doing some walking. Dress for the weather and bring your own lunch. Most of the tours take a full day, leaving at 9 AM and not getting back until 5 PM.

If you do not have time for a tour, just stop in at the centre for information. While at the forestry centre, ask about the sponges that have been made from wood. A dry sponge is very flat but once water is added, it expands to about three times its previous size.

# Port McNeill to Port Alice

## PORT MCNEILL

Back headed north and west on Highway 19, you come to the Nimpkish Fish Hatchery and then you cross the wide Nimpkish River on a long bridge. As you do so, you might want to imagine what it was like on July 19, 1792, when Captain George Vancouver anchored his ship, the *Discovery*, a short distance downstream at the mouth of the river at 10 PM. In the morning he awoke to find that his ship was near a large Native village. The Natives brought over a number of sea otter skins, which traded for sheet copper and blue cloth.

Then you leave the Nimpkish Valley and in 4 kilometres (2.4 miles) you reach the turn-off into Port McNeill. Follow Campbell Way into town and as you start down the hill, look to the right for a small park that contains a war memorial cairn.

This park is part of a demonstration forest. To get to the parking lot and administration building, turn onto McNeill Road. In the park itself you can wander among the small trees and read what type each is. Depending on the logging situation, you can take a longer tour through the adjacent forest.

As you continue down the hill on Campbell Way, you can see Broughton Strait ahead. Follow the road to the ferry and the marina. Just to the right are the tourist information booth and a small park where you can sit on benches or on the lawn and look out over the marina and the water. In the park there is a relic from logging days gone by—a 1938 Washington steam donkey.

*Steam donkey, Port McNeill*

A ferry from here links Port McNeill to Alert Bay on Cormorant Island and to Sointula on Malcolm Island. The ferry makes a round trip every two hours. *Note:* You can leave your vehicle behind if you are planning only to visit Alert Bay, because you can walk all around the town in half a day.

# CORMORANT ISLAND

Cormorant Island is at the top end of Johnstone Strait, where it meets Broughton Strait, and is separated from Queen Charlotte Strait by much larger Malcolm Island. The village of Alert Bay is the centre of the Kwakwa'ka'wakw (formerly called 'Kwakiutl') First Nations. It was here that Natives of this group traditionally gathered during the salmon-fishing season. Local Nimpkish Natives also used the island as a burial ground.

The island was named for the paddle-sloop *HM Cormorant* in 1846 and the village was given the name 'Alert' in 1858, after a corvette stationed off the northwest coast at the time. A permanent settlement was established in the 1870s when two pioneers began a small fish saltery. The operators employed local Nimpkish Natives but discovered that they would return to their homes whenever they wished, as the idea of a steady work week was a foreign concept to them.

In 1882, a cannery was built. When the Canadian Pacific Railway was completed in 1887, linking southwestern BC to the rest of Canada, Alert Bay began supplying the growing populations of Victoria and Vancouver with canned salmon. Fur traders stopped here for supplies, as did gold miners on their way to Alaska.

Today the community is one-half Native and one-half non-Native. It is often called 'the Crossroads of the North' because water traffic travelling up and down among the islands between Vancouver Island and the mainland stops in here for fuel, supplies or just to gossip.

When you dock, you begin by heading up to Front Street. Along the street you go past a nineteenth-century Anglican Church, a historic cemetery, a marina and a cultural centre. Stroll along the boardwalk and natural trails in Gator Gardens, an ecological reserve where there are giant hemlock, redcedar and Douglas-fir trees. That moss hanging from the trees is called 'old man's beard.' It is high in protein and can be boiled and eaten. By the way, the name 'Gator' came from the opinion that the area is much like the Florida Everglades.

Be sure to visit the U'Mista Cultural Centre, which contains a museum that houses a fine collection on Native art and artifacts from 'the Christmas Tree Potlatch' of 1921.

## The Christmas Tree Potlatch

*In 1921, one of the wealthiest potlatches in Native history—called 'the Christmas Tree Potlatch' because of when it was held—took place on Village Island, a small island north of Johnstone Strait and about 20 kilometres (12 miles) east of Malcolm Island.*

*About ten thousand dollars' worth (at 1921 prices) in canoes, gas-boats, clothes, blankets, pool tables, sewing-machines, bureaus, beds, trunks, flour and sugar was given away. However, though it was done in secret, word got out to the Indian Agent. Gifts were seized and over 80 Natives were summoned to court. The trial took place at Alert Bay in March 1922, with lawyers coming from Vancouver to defend the accused. The court agreed to the lawyers' request that if the chiefs gave up their gifts from the potlatch and stopped the practice, they could go free. The chiefs were allowed a month to decide and those who agreed were set free; those who did not were sentenced to a jail term in Vancouver.*

(Also see the Quadra Island section in Chapter 8). These people are working hard to preserve their heritage. The centre is used to teach Native children their history and traditional dances. Members of the community, as well as having potlatches among themselves to mark special occasions, often also demonstrate traditional potlatches and various dances at the cultural centre for the education and enjoyment of tourists. The centre is open Monday to Friday from 9 AM to 5 PM. During the summer it is also open on Sundays and holidays from noon until 5 PM.

It was not until around 1890 that the elaborate totem poles that we know today began to appear at Alert Bay. There are many beautifully carved poles throughout the village, especially at the museum, and at the burial grounds.

The second tallest totem pole in the world is at Alert Bay. (It used to be the tallest until a taller one was carved for the Commonwealth Games in Victoria in 1994.) It is 52.7 metres (173 feet) tall and was made from a 49.7-metre (163-foot) redcedar log donated by the Rayonier Company, with a 3-metre (10-foot) extension added. It was carved in 1973 by five people: Mrs. Billy Cook, Adam and William Matilpi, Benjamin Dick and his son, also named Benjamin. There are 22 different figures on it and at the top there is a sun symbol.

## MALCOLM ISLAND

Malcolm Island, at the southern end of Queen Charlotte Strait, is separated from Vancouver Island by Broughton Strait. Most of the island is privately owned.

In the 1890s, a group of Finnish coal miners were fed up with working in the mines and wanted a more idyllic life. They began a temperance society and brought in a Finnish writer who wanted to form a Finnish community with a Utopian vision. They formed the Kalevan Kansa Colonization Company Ltd. and, after signing an agreement with the government, moved onto Malcolm Island during 1901 and 1902. Each man received 32.4 hectares (80 acres), which had to be improved over seven years before he could get the actual title to the land.

More Finns arrived and shelters were quickly set up. They named their settlement Sointula, which means 'place of harmony' in their native tongue. But many of the immigrants were inexperienced in building a community from the forest. To raise money, they sent logs to Vancouver, but the costs were high and the prices low. The same was true for fish sales, especially since they could not afford to build a cannery. Because of a lack of pasture, their cows were taken across to Vancouver Island. Every day someone would go over and milk them and bring the milk back to the island. As more people arrived and were accepted into the settlement without the cash to pay for their membership in the company, the debt of the community increased.

During one meeting at the end of January 1903, a fire broke out in the community meeting hall. Eleven people died, with more being injured. Discord began to appear, but the Finns still continued to build their community. In the fall of 1904, the community leader put in a bid on a government contract to build bridges over the Seymour and Capilano rivers in North Vancouver. Although community members tried to discourage him, he insisted that the bountiful forests of Malcolm Island would ensure success and lead to more contracts.

However, he had failed to count in costs for other materials and the work was done at a loss. Many of the community members were disillusioned and abandoned their 'Utopia' after this misadventure. In March 1905, the community sawed more lumber, to be marketed to help pay the interest on their mortgage and to buy clothing for the colony. Their creditors were impatient, however, and when they found out the location of the lumber in North Vancouver (where the Finns hoped to sell it), they confiscated it and thereby sealed the end of the Kalevan Kansa Colonization Company Ltd., which by this point had run out of both money and enthusiasm.

Some of the ex-members stayed on the island and farmed or fished or worked in logging camps. In 1909 a co-operative store was built and when it burned down, the Sointula Co-operative Store took its place in 1933. Commercial fishing became a good source of revenue and soon people of other nationalities came to the island as well.

If you look around, you can still find signs of the first settlers. Visit the museum in the schoolhouse off First Street to see some original Finnish books. As you explore the island, watch for saunas and old farmhouses, and notice that many of the gravestones have a hammer and sickle engraved on them.

Although the Co-op Store has an old-world atmosphere, you can nevertheless pick up modern groceries and gas. It is closed on Sundays and is open only until noon on Mondays. The rest of the week it is open from 9:30 AM to 5:30 PM.

If you wish to camp on the island, turn left on Kaleva Road from the ferry dock. Signs from here direct you to Bere Point Regional Park on Bere Point Road. A right turn on Kaleva Road would take you to the hamlet of Mitchel Bay. If you came without a vehicle, you can rent a bicycle at Choyces in Sointula, on the right before Kaleva Road.

## PORT ALICE

*Port Alice*

Return to Port McNeill. Stop at the tourist information booth to pick up a forestry map if you plan to explore some of the logging roads around Port Alice. Then go back to Highway 19 and turn right. In 3.7 kilometres (2.3 miles) from the junction, look to the left for a large green sign that reads, 'Welcome to Port McNeill Managed Forests, West Forest Products Ltd.' To see

*Wharf at Port Alice*

the world's largest known burl—a lump that grows on a tree after a natural disturbance of the cambium layer—turn right onto the gravel logging road across from the sign. Just as you turn, you can already see it in front of you, with the road dividing around it. It has been removed from the base of the tree where it was found growing in 1976, at the head of the Benson River, about 30 kilometres (20 miles) to the south of here. Park on the left and watch out for logging trucks as you walk over to take a closer look.

The huge burl is very dusty because of the trucks driving past it but it is nonetheless very impressive. It is 13.7 metres (45 feet) in circumference and weighs about 20 tonnes (22 tons). It comes from a 79.5-metre (261-foot) high spruce tree that was 350 years old at the time.

Back on the highway, in 15.6 kilometres (9.7 miles) from the burl you arrive at a stop sign where you turn left onto the Port Alice Highway to head for 'the Gateway to the West Coast.' Just after you turn up this paved highway through the forest, you come to Beaver Lake on your right. There is a picnic site here and, if you want to do a little hiking, go to the left side of the road (across the highway from the lake) to walk the self-guiding Beaver Lake Trail through a demonstration forest.

You cross Waukwaas Creek #2 at kilometre 7.5 (mile 4.7) and Waukwaas Creek #1 at kilometre 8.0 (mile 5.0) and then kilometre 12.4 (mile 7.7) brings you to a pull-out to the right. From here on a clear day you can see Broughton Strait, Queen Charlotte Strait, Malcolm Island and the Pulteney Point Lighthouse.

Then you cross the Marble River, with a recreation site on the right at the end of the bridge. You can launch a boat to the left of the bridge to get onto Alice Lake. Marble River flows from Alice Lake to Rupert Inlet, a distance of 9.6 kilometres

**Moving a Town** *The original Port Alice was established in 1917 at the Whalen Pulp and Paper Company mill site farther up Neroutsos Inlet. The town was built by the Whalen brothers, who named it after their mother. Over the years the mill changed hands often and it was while it was owned by the Rayonier Company in the 1960s that the decision was made to move the town.*

*The new Port Alice was begun at its present site on Rumble Beach in 1964. In a province where instant towns sprang up on a regular basis, this new settlement became the province's first 'instant municipality' on June 16, 1965. The change in residence was completed in 1968, with all the buildings at the old site being either moved or destroyed.*

(6.0 miles). Be careful around this river, however—it is extremely fast and dangerous.

After the Marble River, watch for black bears along the highway as it winds its way around many calm ponds, at first climbing and then descending into Port Alice at kilometre 30.1 (mile 18.7).

The tall welcome sign has a carved eagle on top of each of its two posts: one eagle is perching and the other is in flight. You are on Marine Drive as you come into the village, with Neroutsos Inlet on your right. Surrounded by forests and mountains and spread out along the shore of the inlet, Port Alice overlooks the islands out in the water. The settlement has a small marina, a boat launch, a beach and a picnic area.

Continue through the town to visit the mill where Port Alice began. As you leave the outskirts of the town, there is a picnic area on the inlet. As you proceed, be aware that the curving shore road to the mill is subject to debris slides during rainstorms.

In 4.4 kilometres (2.7 miles) from Port Alice, you reach the mill site, where there is a dock from which you can launch a boat. The first pulp was produced at this site in August 1918. When the town was here, it had 50 homes and a hotel.

Past the mill there is a series of logging roads that will take you around the southern tip of the inlet to various points on Quatsino Sound and to the Pacific Ocean. Or you can turn off and drive around Victoria Lake and on to the southern part of Alice Lake and from there back to the Port Alice Highway. Keep a watch for logging activity.

# Fort Rupert to Port Hardy

## FORT RUPERT

When you return to Highway 19 from Port Alice, turn left and go for 11.6 kilometres (7.2 kilometres) until you reach the Fort Rupert Road. Turn right here and in 1.4 kilometres (0.9 miles) turn right again when you get to the stop sign at Bing Road. (To the left the road goes back to the highway and Port Hardy.) When you get to Beaver Harbour Road, turn left to end up at Beaver Harbour and Fort Rupert.

Fort Rupert was established in 1849 by the Hudson's Bay Company on Beaver Harbour. They wanted to protect and mine the coal in the area. It was to be a 'super' fortification, built to be the strongest fortress in the west because of the nearby Nahwittie Native Band, which was known for its fierceness. Captain W.H. MacNeill, after whom Port McNeill is named, was put in charge of the construction.

The 5.5-metre (18-foot) high stockade was made of logs brought from Alaska and sunk deep into the ground. Bastions with cannons were spaced along it. The main gate was recessed so that visitors had to walk between two bastion-guarded palisade walls to reach it and all activity there could be monitored.

Although the Natives in the area had not previously settled on the shores of the harbour, once the fort was constructed, members of the powerful and bloodthirsty local Kwakwa'ka'wakw Band arrived to trade. They set up their longhouses on the shore and called their village Ku-Kultz. Inside the fort there were about a dozen company employees and their Native wives. Outside the post there were about one thousand Natives.

The post became the first coal producer on Vancouver Island, with miners being brought over from England. The fort soon became home to the miners and a trading post for the Natives. Robert Dunsmuir worked in the mines here when he first came from Scotland in 1851 (see Chapter 5).

Eventually, because of disgruntled miners and diminishing coal, the mine failed and the post settled in to fur trading. The company sold the post to its factor (agent), Robert Hunt, in 1873. He traded furs for a few years until a fire wiped out the fort in 1889. He then built a store, which he ran

## The Fate of the Three Deserters

In Victoria, two brothers, Charles and George Wishart, and a companion, Fred Watkins, jumped ship and stowed away on the Hudson's Bay Company's England. The England was headed for Fort Rupert to load up with coal and then bound for California, where new gold-fields had been discovered. The three men wanted a free ride to the fields.

At Fort Rupert, several angry miners agreed to join them on their trip to California. However, another company ship, the Beaver, also dropped anchor at the harbour. Thinking that it was after them, the three deserters fled into the forest. When the Beaver had sailed, word was sent to the men that, because of the hostile Natives, it was not safe in the woods, so they should come out.

The men ignored the warning and refused to return to the post. A few days later, three Nahwittie braves discovered the hiding men. The deserters began waving an axe, shouting and throwing stones, hoping to scare them off. Instead, angered by their actions, the Natives chased them into the woods and hacked them to death.

Two company ships hurried to the scene. When asked to surrender the murderers, the Native band refused to do so. Instead they all fled and the men from the ships burned their village. The next summer, there was a battle in which several Natives were killed and their new village was burned. Finally, when a reward was offered for the capture of the braves, the band asked them to surrender. They refused. Some time later, band members came to the fort bearing three bodies.

Years later it came to light that while two of the accused were slain by band members, one had escaped. To collect the rest of the reward, band members had killed one of their slaves and taken his body to the post, pretending that it was the third brave.

until the Cadwalladers (partly his descendants) took it over. It no longer exists.

Return to Highway 19 via Bing Road. Just after regaining the highway, you come to the Bear Cove Highway on your right—it goes to the terminal for the ferry up the Inside Passage to Prince Rupert.

At this junction there is a sign with carved bears on its top that welcomes you to Port Hardy. Continue along Highway 19 for 1.3 kilometres (0.8 miles) from the sign and turn left onto the road to the Quatse River Hatchery and Coal Harbour.

## COAL HARBOUR

To visit the Quatse River Hatchery, turn left when you reach Bing Road again, 1 kilometre (0.6 mile) from the highway.

The road to Coal Harbour is paved, with a few slight curves and hills. At kilometre 8.2 (mile 5.1) you come to a Y in the road. Turn right for Coal Harbour. The road to the left goes to the former Island Copper Mines, once known as 'the Utah Mines.' The open-pit mine closed at the beginning of 1996 and when measured, the pit was 2.4 kilometres by 1.2 kilometres (1.5 miles by 0.7 mile) across and 400 metres (1320 feet) deep. The site is closed to the public until the land has been reclaimed.

*Whale bones, Coal Harbour*

Continuing towards Coal Harbour, you reach Quatsino First Nations Village, which has beautiful carvings, in 4.8 kilometres (3 miles) from the Y. Several of the carvings are in memory of deceased family members and friends.

Just past the village you arrive at Coal Harbour. Its name comes from a deposit of coal found in the area in the 1880s. The beautiful harbour itself is to the left as you drive through town on Coal Harbour Road. Go to the dock at the end of it. All the land at the dock is privately owned, so park in the parking lot.

Just before the dock, Harbour Road goes to your right. Turn onto it and in about one block you come to a huge whale bone on the left side of the road. This 6-metre (20-foot) lower jawbone comes from a blue whale, the largest species of animal in the world. This whale can grow to be 29 metres (95 feet) in length and weigh about 135 tonnes (150 tons).

Beside the bone there are a whaling gun or harpoon and an anchor. These relics are symbols of an industry that operated here for twenty years, beginning in 1947. A nearby cairn is dedicated to the people who served at Royal Canadian Air Force Station Coal Harbour during the Second World War. The RCAF seaplane base and reconnaissance station established here operated for two and

Coal Harbour

one-half years patrolling Canada's west coast with long-range flying boats.

You can take a water taxi from Coal Harbour to Winter Harbour if you do not want to travel the gravel logging road described later in this chapter.

When you come back to Highway 19, you have the option to stop in at Port Hardy to do your shopping or make inquiries at the tourist information booth before continuing. Since the road you are on crosses the highway, passes Hardy Bay

Whale gun, Coal Harbour

and goes into the town via Roosevelt Avenue and Hardy Bay Road, you can take that route, but the main highway also goes there. To skip Port Hardy (which is covered in more detail at the end of this chapter), just turn left onto the highway.

## HOLBERG, CAPE SCOTT & WINTER HARBOUR

Just 0.7 kilometres (0.4 miles) up the highway from the Coal Harbour turn-off, turn left (to your right if you are leaving Port Hardy southbound on the highway) to go to Holberg.

The road starts out paved but soon becomes gravel, though it is well signposted all the way to Holberg. At kilometre 6.9 (mile 4.3) go left and up the hill when you reach a Y. This road is wide but bumpy, with potholes. In 13.3 kilometres (8.2 miles) from the highway you get glimpses of Kains Lake to your right through the trees. Just after that is 'the Tree of Lost Soles,' also known as 'the Shoe Tree,' beside the road on your right.

The Shoe Tree began when one of Holberg's residents, tired of the boring drive into Port Hardy, decided to liven it up by nailing a pair of her son's running shoes to this tree. Since then, many other people have followed suit.

If you wish to put your shoe(s) on the tree, you are going to have to climb quite high because the trunk is full for a long ways up and a log lying across the base of the tree is also full. One pair of shoes is halfway up the tree.

By 22.5 kilometres (14 miles) from the highway, the road is following along Nahwitti Lake. There are side roads down to the lake if you wish to spend some time camping, swimming or boating before continuing. A further 20 kilometres (12.4 miles) from the lake you reach Holberg.

Danish settlers came to the Cape Scott area in 1896 and began farming. Their efforts were successful but they had little access to markets where they could sell their excess and buy items that they could not produce for themselves. Most of them left but the few people remaining gathered together to start a community that they named 'Holberg,' after a figure in Danish literature, at the head of what became Holberg Inlet. By 1916, however, only three families were left.

In 1942, a floating logging camp was built here and it grew to become the largest floating town in the world. It was 400 metres (0.25 mile) long and the homes on it had power, hot and cold water and gardens. The town had a fire department, a store, a pool hall, a community hall and a machine shop. Fourteen years later, a permanent town was begun on the shore.

If you have been doing your own cooking and you are getting tired of it, stop in at The Scarlet Ibis Restaurant. Although it is the only restaurant in Holberg, it does not scrimp on either tastiness or portions.

To continue on towards Cape Scott Provincial Park and/or Winter Harbour, head northwest, following the signs that begin past the Western Forest Products office. In spite of the sign that warns 'Elephant Crossing' at kilometre 4.1 (mile 2.5), there are no elephants to worry about. One story has it that the reference to elephants comes from a humourous comparison between them and big, slow-moving logging trucks. Another says that if you drink and drive you might see pink elephants along this road.

When you reach the stop sign shortly after the elephant crossing, you can continue ahead to the southwest, to go straight to Winter Harbour. If you are in the mood for some hiking out to the ocean, turn right towards Cape Scott Provincial Park instead.

The road has been deactivated by the forest service and is not maintained. There are potholes and rocks to negotiate and there is grass growing between the ruts. Watch for bears, deer and other wildlife. In 2.8 kilometres (1.7 miles) you come to a logging road that is still in use. Turn left onto it and in about 1 kilometre (0.5 mile), turn left again and from here there are signs to direct you the rest of the way to Cape Scott.

After you cross the San Josef River, continue straight at the first junction and at the second you have the option to turn left onto Ronning Main if you want to go to Raft Cove Provincial Park (there is a sign). It is about 12 kilometres (7.5 miles) to the parking area. From there you can hike to the cove, which has 1.5 kilometres (1 mile) of sandy beach.

Continuing on the road to Cape Scott, you cross the San Josef River again and come to a small sign for the Ronning Gardens on your right. Turn into the lane and go to the parking area. Walk back a very short distance along the lane to a trail that leads into the gardens. Step over the barrier of stones to begin your stroll.

After ten minutes of walking through the rainforest along this part of the old Cape Scott wagon road, you are suddenly in an oasis of tropical plants. It is really a shock to see giant sequoia growing this far north.

Shoe Tree, Port Hardy

Because the gardens are on the alluvial plain of the San Josef River, there are lots of mosquitoes. Wear long pants and a long-sleeved shirt or jacket and use insect repellent so that you will be free to enjoy the 2-hectare (5-acre garden) in peace.

The creator of the gardens, a man named Ronning who was one of the original settlers from Denmark, spent almost fifty years ordering exotic species to plant and looking after them. After he died in the 1960s, the rainforest started to take over again.

Then, in the early 1980s, the present owners, Ron and Julie Moe, bought the property and began to clean it up. So far they have identified over one hundred different shrubs and trees and most of them are labelled.

You are welcome to visit whether or not the owners are there and there is no charge to visit the gardens—the owners simply ask that you leave everything as you found it and take any of your garbage with you. If you would like to contribute to the gardens, there is a donation box.

In 5.5 kilometres (3.4 miles) from the lane to the gardens you reach the turnoff for the San Josef Recreation Site. You can stop here or continue past the boat launch to the edge of Cape Scott Provincial Park where there is a parking lot for the trailheads.

Encompassing 15,000 hectares (37,000 acres) of wilderness, Cape Scott Provincial Park has black bear, deer, cougar and elk roaming through it. In the air there are peregrine falcons and other birds, and out in the water there are sea lions, seals and otters.

One of the easiest hikes is a 30–45-minute trip to San Josef Bay, while other trails go to lakes, along the San Josef River and to Cape Scott itself. Along the trails, remnants of the area's past that you might encounter include a boiler, a bathtub, an abandoned farmstead, a stove, a telegraph line, a Caterpillar tractor and old buildings.

Note that only experienced hikers should attempt the 25.7-kilometre (16-mile), two-day return-trip hike to Cape Scott. The trail can be muddy, there are wild animals to contend with, the weather can change at any time and there are no facilities or services.

Cape Scott was given its name by James Strange, after his fur-trading partner, David Scott, in 1786. Because the northwestern tip of Vancouver Island is open to the open ocean on both the north and the west, stormy weather and rough water have sunk many ships. The area receives as much as 5100 millimetres (200 inches) of rain annually, making it one of the wettest regions in North America. When a storm blows in, the winds can reach 160 kilometres per hour (100 miles per hour).

Back at the junction with the road to Winter Harbour, turn to the southwest on DND Road to head towards Winter Harbour. The route has plenty of signs, so you are not likely to get lost. In 9.2 kilometres (5.7 miles) you reach a junction, where you turn left. (If you went straight ahead, you would come to the site of an old Canadian Forces Base but you would not be able to get into the site because of a locked gate.) The village of Winter Harbour is about 20 kilometres (12 miles) down the road from the junction, via S 730 and South Main. Since you are on gravel logging roads, drive with your headlights on.

For years, Winter Harbour has been used as a port for commercial fishers seeking shelter from winter storms out on the ocean. In the early 1930s, settlers here lived on floats. They logged in the winter and fished in the summer. As the community grew, houses were built on cleared land on the shore. In 1960, a tidal wave, the result of an earthquake in Chile, inflicted much damage on the small settlement and four years later an earthquake in Alaska caused the water to rise again.

Incidentally, Winter Harbour is closer to Asia than is any other occupied place on Vancouver Island.

If you want to spend the night, you can choose from Kwasksista Park, which has twelve campsites, and a bed-and-breakfast. The village also has a store and a cafe. For exercise, you can walk along the boardwalk. If you wish to take a quiet, relaxing stroll through an old-growth forest, watch for the set of stairs along the road between the store and the dock. You can walk it in anywhere between ten minutes and thirty minutes, depending on how thoroughly you want to enjoy it.

Return to Holberg by the same route. (While maps suggest that you could take South Main the whole way back, it is recommended that you take DND Road because parts of South Main are too narrow and busy with logging trucks to be safe.)

## PORT HARDY

From Holberg, return to Highway 19. For the easiest route into Port Hardy, the largest town on northern Vancouver Island, simply turn left and follow the highway straight into town. Just 2.1 kilometres (1.3 miles) from the junction you reach a T intersection. The Rotary Park and the beach are in front of you, along with a huge welcome sign with a bear and a fish on it. Turn to the right to reach the tourist information centre.

At Carrot Park, ahead and to the left, is the sculpture known as The Mile Zero Trans Carrot. Since 1897, each prospective government had 'dangled a carrot' in front of north-island voters by promising to build a road across the 160 kilometres (100 miles) of wilderness known as 'the Incredible Gap' that separated the northerners from the road network to the south.

After each election, the residents of the northern community waited hopefully for the promised road. But it never came and finally they launched 'the Carrot Campaign' in the late 1970s to let the nation know of their plight. The government of the day relented and the north island received 'the rest of the carrot' and this sculpture was created to commemorate the success of the campaign. The 'trans' part of

*Port Hardy carrot*

the sculpture's name means 'across' (as in 'trans-Atlantic'), relating to the Incredible Gap.

Just across the road from the carrot sculpture, in front of the North Shore Inn, there is a propeller from the *SS Themis*. The 82-metre (270-foot) steel freighter hit the Crocker Rocks in Gordon Channel during a storm in December 1906 and was wrecked.

Having toured all over Vancouver Island, you can continue on up through the beautiful Inside Passage to Prince Rupert by ferry from Port Hardy. Or you can head for home, along the way perhaps stopping in to revisit a few favourite places or setting off to explore beyond the confines of this book.

# FURTHER READING

Andersen, Doris. *Evergreen Islands*. Vancouver: Whitecap Books Ltd. 1979, 1985.

Bryan, Liz and Jack. *Country Roads*. Vancouver: Sunflower Publications Ltd., 1991.

Bryan, Liz and Jack. *Backroads of British Columbia*. Vancouver: Sunflower Publications Ltd., 1975.

Downs, Art. Editor. *Pioneer Days in British Columbia*. Vol. 1 & 2. Surrey: Heritage House and the Authors, 1973, 1977.

Gibson, Nancy and John Whittaker. *Lone Pine Picnic Guide to British Columbia*. Edmonton: Lone Pine Publishing, 1989.

King, Jane. *British Columbia Handbook*. California: Moon Publications, Inc., 1989.

Kramer, Pat. *B.C. For Free*. Vancouver: Whitecap Books Ltd., 1992.

McKeever, Harry. *Vancouver Island*. Vancouver: Whitecap Books Ltd., 1981.

McKeever, Harry. *An Explorer's Quide to British Columbia*. San Francisco: Chronicle Books, 1977, 1978, 1982.

Nanton, Isabel and Mary Simpson. *Adventuring in British Columbia*. Vancouver: Douglas & McIntyre Ltd., 1991.

Obee, Bruce. *The Pacific Rim Explorer*. Vancouver: Whitecap Books. Ltd., 1986.

Pattison, Ken. *Milestones on Vancouver Island*. Victoria: Pattison Ventures Ltd., 1973, 1974, 1978, 1983, 1986.

Short, Steve and Rosemary Neering. *In the Path of the Explorers*. Vancouver: Whitecap Books Ltd., 1992.

Watmough, Don. *West Coast of Vancouver Island*. Vancouver: Special Interest Publications, 1984.

# INDEX

# More Lone Pine titles to help you discover the great outdoors.

## SEASHORE OF BRITISH COLUMBIA
### by Ian Sheldon
A spectacular guide to the plants, animals, shells, crawlies and creepies of the majestic Pacific seashore. Ian Sheldon's illustrations and easy, natural writing style set this guide "head and fins" above the others. Fascinating to read even if you never get near the water.
ISBN 1-55105-163-X • 4.25" x 8.25", softcover, 192 pages, full-colour illustrations throughout, $15.95 CDN.

## BEST HIKES AND WALKS OF SOUTHWESTERN BRITISH COLUMBIA
### by Dawn Hanna
The author, a well-known journalist, covers 77 spectacular hikes, all within about three hours of Vancouver. Notes on natural history and aboriginal lore are combined with important hiking information.
ISBN 1-55105-095-1 • 4.25" x 8.25", softcover, 360 pages, maps and colour photos throughout, $19.95 CDN.

## BACKROADS OF SOUTHWESTERN BRITISH COLUMBIA
### by Joan Donaldson-Yarmey
Discover the best of British Columbia's well-kept secrets with this thorough guide to the beautiful southwest of the province. Designed to allow you to complete any trip within one day or combine them to form great back-country road trips.
ISBN 1-55105-097-8 • 5.5" x 8.5", softcover, 168 pages, B&W photos throughout, $12.95 CDN.

## BACKROADS OF SOUTHERN INTERIOR BRITISH COLUMBIA
### by Joan Donaldson-Yarmey
Explore the best-ever back-country getaways and hidden treasures. Take a trip from the Rockies to the Coquihalla, through the Kootenays and the Okanagan. The perfect vacation planner.
ISBN 1-55105-070-6 • 5.5" x 8.5", softcover, 224 pages, B&W photos throughout, $14.95 CDN.

## CANADIAN ROCKIES ACCESS GUIDE
### by John Dodd and Gail Helgason
This essential guide for exploring the Rockies includes 106 day hikes, plus information on backpacking, boating, camping, cycling, fishing, golf and rainy-day activities. This is the most comprehensive guide to travel and recreational opportunities in Banff, Jasper, Kootenay, Yoho, Waterton and Kananaskis parks.
ISBN 1-55105-176-1 • 5.5" x 8.5", softcover, 400 pages, full-colour maps and photos throughout, $19.95 CDN.

### CANADA
#206, 10426-81 Avenue
Edmonton, Alberta T6E 1X5
Ph: (403) 433-9333 or (800) 661-9017
Fax: (403) 433-9646 or (800) 424-7173
E-mail: info@lonepinepublishing.com
Web site: www.lonepinepublishing.com

### USA
1901 Raymond Avenue SW, Suite C
Renton, Washington 98055
Ph: (425) 204-5965 or (800) 518-3541
Fax: (425) 204-6036 or (800) 548-1169
E-mail: heleni@wolfnet.com
Web site: www.lonepinepublishing.com